CLASSIC BUS

YEARBOOK – 2

Edited by Gavin Booth

IAN ALLAN Publishing

CONTENTS

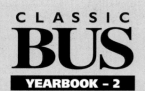

First published 1996
ISBN 0 7110 2446 4

All rights reserved. No part of this book may be
reproduced or transmitted in any form or by any
means, electronic or mechanical, including
photocopying, recording or by any information
storage and retrieval system, without permission
from the Publisher in writing.

© Ian Allan Ltd 1996
Published by Ian Allan Publishing

an imprint of Ian Allan Ltd, Terminal House,
Station Approach, Shepperton, Surrey TW17 8AS
Printed by Ian Allan Printing Ltd,
Coombelands House, Coombelands Lane,
Addlestone, Surrey KT15 1HY

INTRODUCTION

THE SUCCESS of the first *Classic Bus Yearbook,* published in 1995, encouraged Ian Allan Ltd to produce this second edition. We have tried to make it a natural extension to the bi-monthly *Classic Bus* magazine, with a mix of articles and photo-features by some of the best-known names in transport journalism and photography.

So we have Michael H C Baker recalling a wartime London bus journey in the much-loved STL type AEC Regents; Thomas W W Knowles remembering his formative years in the Potteries area; Alan Millar on the many and varied names chosen for bus chassis and bodies over the years; Jasper Pettie looking back sadly at buses that slipped through his grasp; Robert E Jowitt getting misty-eyed over Bournemouth trolleybuses and contemporary girlfriends; Roy Marshall setting forth in 1951 on a journey of discovery from Great Yarmouth to Plymouth; Frank Rowlands on Bristol REs in New Zealand; David Stanier on Daimler's Freeline model; John Dunabin looks back to the heyday of coach trips between London and the coast, and Harry Postlethwaite describes the wartime scene in West Cumberland. Oh yes, and I admit, reluctantly it must be said, that Leyland didn't always get things right.

There are photo-features too: R D Okill's photos taken in Scotland in 1939, including an amazing and rare prewar colour photograph and S J Butler illustrates buses still in use after their main lives were over;

'Classic Blunderbus' is a popular feature of *Classic Bus*, describing some of the real duffers that have been built for service in the UK; for the *Yearbook,* Alan Millar takes a positive view and describes a well-deserved Classic Wonderbus – the Bristol Lodekka.

Back by popular demand is the 'Classic Bus Alphabet', a light-hearted look at the world of classic buses, and the preserved vehicles that feature in our Peter Durham cover photos are described in the feature 'Cover Story'.

If you enjoy the book, remember that a similar mix can be found every two months in *Classic Bus* magazine, available from bookstalls and news-stands throughout the UK.

Gavin Booth
Edinburgh

Front cover: **Peter Durham's fine studies of preserved buses are a regular feature of** *Classic Bus* **magazine. The classic lines of the London Transport Routemaster show up well on RM254, new in 1960. Geoff Rixon describes RM254's life and restoration on pages 74/5.**

Back cover: **Two more Peter Durham studies of preserved buses. Two fairly unusual buses from the much-missed David MacBrayne fleet: a 1949 Thornycroft Nippy with 20-seat Croft body and a 1949 Maudslay Marathon III with 35-seat Park Royal body. Read about them on page 104. Alan Roberts' preserved ex-Jones, Aberbeeg, Leyland Tiger Cub/Weymann was new in 1958. Read about it on pages 86/7.**

Title page: **Recalling Leyland's happier days, a Ribble Tiger Cub coach with Burlingham Seagull body seen on an excursion when new. Ribble was a dedicated Leyland customer for many years, but like many other operators it turned to other makes when Leyland's ambitions created problems in the 1960s and 1970s.**

Right: **An Olympian, Jim, but not as we know it. See page 45.**
Alan Millar

By STL to the ZOO

'Great Bus Journeys of the World' is an occasional feature in *Classic Bus* magazine. MICHAEL H C BAKER describes a 1944 London journey

London Transport ST615, Croydon (TC) based, at the 59B terminus at Thornton Heath Pond. This bus was from the main production batch of STs, delivered from 1930.

Michael H C Baker

THE JOURNEY in question took place in the summer of 1944 and our destination was Regent's Park Zoo. This was long before the days of safari parks, David Attenborough and a general awareness that zoos might not altogether be a good thing. So we looked forward to the expedition with unalloyed joy, not least on account of the journey by double-deck bus. Then, as now, I'm a sucker for any form of transport – excepting air, with or without a parachute – but what was particularly appealing about a journey over practically the whole length of the 159 was that it would most likely be in London Transport's very nearly most up-to-date double-decker, an STL. This claim needs a certain amount of qualification, but we'll come to that later.

My friend Malcolm's granny lived in Green Lane, Thornton Heath. We spent quite a lot of time there for Malcolm's father was away in the war serving with the RAF as a navigator in a Liberator bomber, and his mother spent what seemed to me – and no doubt much more obviously to Malcolm – a long time away too, in a sanatorium suffering from tuberculosis. Nobody of course used a private car during the war, even if they owned one, and so we travelled everywhere by public transport.

It was something like eight miles from Thornton Heath to Regent's Park, which may not sound very much, but to a seven-year-old it was an epic journey. We never thought of ourselves as living in the capital, even though Thornton Heath was officially swallowed by it after the war. Green Lane was served by just one bus route, the 159, which ran from the Clock Tower, Thornton Heath, to Camden Town. Green Lane had got its name because that had precisely described it until a few years earlier when there were still fields between Norbury, which was part of London proper, and Thornton Heath. I remember seeing a newsreel of Green Lane in its rural days with an ST passing along it, so it couldn't have been that much earlier, the first ST having entered service with the London General Omnibus Company in 1929. Malcolm's granny lived in a council house dating from the early 1930s, which would have been when the last fields disappeared.

Let us consider the STL. It was an AEC Regent and was London's standard bus in production from the inception of the London Passenger Transport Board in July 1933 until the outbreak of war in September 1939. Its origins went back to the autumn of 1932 when the first Thomas Tilling STL entered service, followed by the first General example in the January of the

following year. STL meant Short Type (ST, its 25ft long predecessor) Lengthened (to 26ft) but apart from this the Tilling and General bodies had little in common. The Tilling version was much the more rounded and, I suppose, the more modern, although it had three windows at the upstairs front and certain other features in common with the Tilling ST, which dated it. The General STL was upright and angular, and managed to squeeze in 60 passengers, which gave them a somewhat top-heavy look. They bore similarities to the Bluebird LTs and STs, but were less well-proportioned.

Sit-up-and-beg

The next development brings us one step away from the standard STL. This was the famous sit-up-and-beg variety – so called because a number subsequently had their petrol engines replaced by diesel ones which necessitated a slight raising of their front ends – familiar to this day for two examples have been preserved. The back was very close to the final version, being elegantly curved, but the front was more upright, sloping back in a straight line from the top of the driver's bulkhead. Croydon had been a Thomas Tilling garage but 22 of its Tilling STLs, and a couple of Manchester Crossleys on loan had been destroyed during the blitz on the night of 10 May 1941, and since then, although a good few Tilling STLs remained, General STs had become the commonest type.

From here on this section of the story takes place several miles above the North Atlantic as I'm writing it on an Icelandair Boeing Husky or something probably called Erik the Red, on its way from Glasgow to Keflavik – some sort of first I would imagine for a Classic Bus contribution. (Actually I was aiming for the editorial headquarters in Edinburgh but braked too late.)

Back to Green Lane and the 159. The final blossoming of the standard STL arrived in 1934, with

the gently-curved front, oil-engined, 56 seats – for many years I assumed that an Act of Parliament decreed all highbridge double-deckers had to have 56 seats. Slight variations continued right up to 1939, the highest numbered being STL2647. The chief external variations that I observed were the arrangement of the front route indicators. Nos 609-958 were identical to the sit-up-and-beg STLs with the ultimate destination below the via and number blinds, then on Nos 1060-1613 it moved above them, and finally from 1614 the number moved to a lighthouse situation in the roof. The gap from 959 to 1059 was filled by country area, forward-entrance vehicles.

The roof number box was a feature almost unique to London Transport, and although it had been used before the STL, it was they who achieved fame far beyond the capital. Whenever a cartoonist wanted to depict a double-deck bus it seemed he would choose an AEC radiator and a roofbox, never mind what the rest looked like, although the late, great Giles depicted an STL more than once with better than photographic accuracy. What probably made the roofbox STL just about immortal was Meccano Ltd which in 1938 from its Binns Road factory in Liverpool marketed it, the first mass-produced, reasonably accurate model bus – even though the livery had nothing to do with London's – to the same scale as its newly-introduced Hornby Dublo trains.

When Dinky Toys were reintroduced in limited numbers after the war we, that is form 5 at Winterbourne Primary School, Norbury, would belt down to Wises, our local dealers, in the hope of obtaining one, pocket money permitting. We might be lucky although they sold out within minutes. I did once heretically swap one for an even rarer Queen Mary on wheels, but I still have three, all bought much later at jumble sales, before the WI and parent teachers associations realised that such things were becoming collectors' items, in much less than pristine condition,

and a mint condition Leyland version. The latter are
much more often come across at swapmeets; they
represent the STD, an all-Leyland TD4 Titan version,
100 of which were produced for London Transport in
1937. Whilst not a perfect STL look-alike it was
nevertheless a commendable attempt by the Leyland
engineers, and a favourite with both drivers and
enthusiasts. Sadly none have survived. To complete the
STL story there were, apart from some early
curiosities, 34 unfrozen STLs brought out during the
war and fitted with a variety of bodies, some
secondhand and some new, austerity versions both

highbridge and lowbridge. Finally 20 more or less
standard Weymann-bodied MkII Regents were
delivered in November 1945; they were numbered
STL2682-2701 and spent their London careers in the
country area. One, STL2692, after further service with
Grimsby, has been beautifully restored to original
London Country condition.

Okay, so now our journey can begin.

Upstairs front seats

The 159 starts some five minutes back from Malcolm's
granny's house, our bus is not very full and we get

front seats upstairs – where else? We're delighted to find that our STL is one of the newest, an FXT-registered one, delivered just before the war. Many of this batch were transferred when almost new from Hanwell to Streatham (tough luck, Hanwell) ousting the LTs which were working the 159 at the time. They had deeper radiators and rear wheel discs and were the most refined of all their breed, although inevitable after the deprivations of the War and four years reduced maintenance, they're not as immaculate as they once were.

The Green Lane district, nestling beneath Norwood Heights was, and is, a rather sedate area inhabited by a nice class of person, a fair proportion of whom lived in bow-windowed, mock-Tudor semi-detacheds, once fiercely derided, now regarded with increasing affection. Leaving Norbury we turn into Streatham High Road, the A23 Brighton Road, and from now on we will encounter more and more bus and tram routes. It would be tedious to list them all but we cannot ignore our best friend, the 59a – the 59 was a large and constantly-changing family – which is also worked by Streatham STLs and has begun its journey at Addiscombe. It will keep us company all the way to Camden Town.

The busiest routes using Streatham High Road are the 16/18 trams. These run from Purley, the southernmost extremity of the London tram system and almost in the country, to the

Embankment. Worked by a variety of types from Thornton Heath and Telford Avenue depots, assisted from time to time by Purley and Brixton Hill, they have the distinction that many of them are Felthams, those magnificent beasts which might have defeated the trolleybus and held the motorbus at bay had London Transport and the times been so inclined.

We climb to Streatham Common. Here, some three years earlier I had last seen an STL with complete prewar destination blinds. Wartime economy decreed the blanking-out of number and ultimate screens, leaving a reduced via one to convey as much as it could. I was only four at the time, but I clearly remember it was a 133, another route which linked the County Borough of Croydon with central London, in this instance Liverpool Street. Some of the first prefabs, temporary bungalows to house those made homeless by bombing, were put up on Streatham Common. Beyond, on the left, we pass our vehicle's home garage with brother STLs parked outside and within. We overtake a Feltham, the conductor lowering its trolley arm, the plough carrier for conduit collection having been inserted into its nether regions. We climb again, up to St Leonards Church where yet more Felthams and much inferior E1s, some dating back to pre-World War 1 days, join us from Tooting.

Heavier traffic

Shops line the road on both sides, traffic grows heavier – buses, trams and commercial vehicles that is, for there are few cars – as we penetrate deeper into the inner suburbs. On past Streatham Hill station, Telford Avenue depot, next door to Brixton Hill where war-damaged and withdrawn E1s, some still without windscreens, are glimpsed, and then comes the long descent to Brixton.

On the right are some once grand mid-Victorian villas with long front gardens, but we're now over Iceland and looking down on a glacier, something seldom seen in Brixton, so I'll stop for the moment.

Where was I, Kevlavik? Ah no, Brixton; the confusion is understandable. It was from the front garden of one of the Victorian villas that my father bought our car. It was a Lanchester 12 and cost £7.10/- (£7.50). He was working in the NAAFI offices in Brixton at the time, spied it from the top of a homeward-bound tram one evening, and next lunchtime, made the dealer an offer he couldn't refuse; goodness knows what sort of living a secondhand car dealer made in the middle of World War 2. The Lanchester car company had been taken over by Daimler following the 1930 slump; Father had been trained as a mechanic by Daimler before World War 1 and had driven the make as a chauffeur in the 1920s. In effect our Lanchester was the smallest in the Daimler range. Dinky Toys made a model of one with a Daimler radiator, but that was about the only

Roofbox STL1644 outside Streatham garage in November 1954.
Michael H C Baker

difference. The dealer let my father have just enough petrol to drive it home to the lock-up garage across the road, and for years I would watch him tinker with it, starting up the engine briefly, using a thimbleful of the precious fluid, until the great day arrived in the summer of 1945 when we made our first expedition in it to Reigate Heath. The most memorable feature, apart from the fabric roof which leaked in heavy rain, was its fluid flywheel. I'm not quite sure just why but Father assured me it was so. We once took it to be repaired at a garage in Lansdowne Road, Croydon, Palmers, which boasted a Rolls-Royce breakdown lorry, but that's another story.

At the bottom of Brixton Hill is Lambeth Town Hall, which always confuses me, yet more trams, the Orange Luxury Coach depot, although it wouldn't have been functioning in 1944, and two completely contrasting bus routes, the 35 which is operated by open staircase, six-wheel LTs from Leyton garage, and the 37, worked from Putney by London's most up-to-date bus, the RT, the latest of which was then little more than two years old. Both have their own voices: the petrol-engined LTs a gasp, with an occasional explosive cough; the RTs a throb, neither much resembling the steady purr of the STL.

Brixton, then as now, was a rackety, somewhat intimidating, but also alluring place with its prison, its street market beside the railway arches, one very high, one quite low bridge spanning the main street, the exotically-named Bon Marche store, the constant rattle of innumerable trams, and what was surely the world's largest motor cycle dealers, painted bright red, just round the corner on both sides of the Stockwell Road, where decades later our Icelandic friends would live – now you see the cunningly worked-in earlier reference.

Deeper into the suburbs

On we go, ever deeper into the inner suburbs, all yellow-grey brick Victoriana, except where the Luftwaffe has created gaps, and we are now at Kennington, within sight of the Oval where Len Hutton's record-breaking 364, scored in August 1938 in the last England v Australia test match before the outbreak of war, is still a topic of conversation. We cross the Victoria and Kensal Green-bound 36 route and run along the edge of Kennington Park. 45 STLs operate the 36, originally all of the Tilling variety, but latterly more modern, standard vehicles have supplanted many of them.

We part company with the 133 bus, and the 18 tram routes, which have kept us company from Norbury; they continue towards the City whilst we turn left, westwards.

At the Imperial War Museum we swing left again, out of Kennington Road, leaving the 16 tram route, and into Lambeth Road. Under the railway bridge carrying the Western Section main line of the Southern Railway into Waterloo station – the most bombed section of railway in the British Isles, the 24 miles between Queens Road, Battersea and Waterloo being attacked 92 times between 1940 and 1945 – and as we pass Lambeth Palace, the home of the Archbishop of Canterbury, and the W H Smith store on the left, suddenly, there across the river is Big Ben and the Houses of Parliament. Even today, 50 years and countless occasions later, it's a view which never fails to thrill.

Over Lambeth Bridge we go, a tug pulling a string of coal barges bound for Battersea Power station steams towards us under Westminster Bridge, its funnel lowered, whilst an almost continuous line of trams, interspersed with several LTs working the 12 and 53, passes above. Beyond is a temporary bailey bridge,

The young Michael on the bonnet of the Baker Lanchester flanked by his Father (right) and Uncle Harry.

Michael H C Baker

'Sit-up-and-beg' STL436 about to cross Lambeth Bridge in the summer of 1949.

Michael H C Baker collection

erected in case any of the bridges across the Thames should be destroyed by the Luftwaffe or the flying bombs, a new terror weapon which was launched in the summer of 1944. I remember being on a bus passing the Swan and Sugar Loaf, South Croydon, when the 'thud' of one falling nearby prompted the conductor to remark ' That's a few less fares for me to bother about,' a piece of black humour which caused considerable offence to several passengers.

Our STL makes its way through the avenue of trees spanning Millbank, past the spot where nowadays MPs are interviewed nightly by TV with a frankness unthinkable in the tight-lipped 1940s. From now on Malcolm and I can hardly contain our excitement as one famous landmark succeeds another. Round Parliament Square – one of the most famous newsreel images of the war is of an STL following a tank there – past Westminster Abbey, St Margarets, then up Whitehall with always a hope of seeing Winston Churchill or at least his cigar emerging from 10 Downing Street – no security gates barring the general public then. A cousin of my Fathers who died not so long ago in her late 90s used to tell me of going to meet her Father who worked for the Crown Agents in Downing Street, by horse bus.

Amongst the 18 routes which traverse Whitehall, we are always on the lookout for number 11s, London's most famous route. As no fewer than 70 buses are required to maintain its two-minute headway (28 STLs from Dalston and 42 LTs, including the magnificent Bluebirds, from Riverside, Hammersmith) we are never disappointed.

We have to use our imaginations as we pass the sombre, khaki-clad sentries outside Horse Guards parade. Easy enough to do for one of my favourite records, played on our wind-up 78 gramophone, is a light baritone singing a number entitled 'The Changing of the Guard' complete with sound effects of cheering crowds. There are photographs in our album that my Father took of the uncrowned Edward VIII at the 1936 Trooping of the colour, and I have been brought up fired by my parents' love of London and its prewar pageantry.

Phoney accent

Out of Whitehall and round Trafalgar Square (an early *Buses Illustrated* featured this as its frontispiece with a wonderfully evocative photograph of an STD in all its prewar, silver-roofed glory amongst the upright Beardmore and Austin taxis and cloche hats). Piccadilly Circus lacks Eros, removed for safe-keeping, and the neon advertising signs, and I never did see the flower seller who was supposed to sit on the steps and introduce 'In Town Tonight' each Saturday evening at 7 o'clock on the BBC Home Service with her cry 'Violets, lovely violets,' in what seemed to me a pretty phoney Cockney accent.

Sweeping up Regent Street and past the 'biggest toy shop in the world' which I didn't get round to entering until I took my own children in the 1970s, and so to Oxford Circus where, then as now, front-engined

Regent Street c1945. STL2363 (note the characteristic upper deck emergency exit) is working the 60, ahead is a D (utility Daimler). Michael H C Baker collection

double-deckers with open rear platforms constantly pass.

Broadcasting House, straight ahead, impresses me both visually and because of the wonders within which reached us via our battery-operated wireless, assisted by an acid-filled accumulator which is recharged at the Victory Garage round the Pond beside the 59 and 59B terminus every week – Richard Murdoch, Kennneth Horne, Sam Costa and Maurice Denham in 'Much Binding in the Marsh' and Uncle Mac and the beautifully modulated voice of David Davies of 'Children's Hour' are my favourites.

Piccadilly Circus in wartime with no Eros, few cars, several taxis, and London buses of the STD, LT and STL families.

A roofbox STL on the 159 and an ST behind Portland Place.
Michael H C Baker

Broadcasting House marks the end of the heart of London although less decisively than the Thames marked its beginning on the approach from the south, the number of bus routes sharing the streets behind Portland Place declining drastically as we approach Regents Park and our destination.

We get out, just as we boarded, a couple of stops short of the 159's terminus. Camden Town, like other never-visited destinations seen on London buses and trams – Stoke Newington, Beresford Square and Plumstead Common for example – sounds to us as exotic as Nova Scotia or Tahiti. Kipling could have written a poem about any of them, Betjeman, of course, did.

So we leave our STL and walk alongside the Regents Canal. Despite growing anticipation of the delights to come, the sea lions jumping for fish, the dignified penguins standing quietly to attention in sloping lines so as not to distract admirers of modern architecture from their wonderful Berthold Lubetkins concrete pool, the tropical smells of the monkey house, the bored lions pacing up and down – I have time to note the only bus route which passes the Zoo entrance, the 74. This is something special for like the

Preserved 'prewar' RT113 at Cobham in April 1995 displaying blinds for the 74 route, which passed the Zoo.

Michael H C Baker

PICTURE POST EVERY WEDNESDAY

PUTNEY HEATH GREEN MAN
BAKER ST MARBLE ARCH
HYDE PARK CORNER
SOUTH KENSINGTON
EARLS COURT PUTNEY

74

FXT288

37 we saw at Brixton it is worked by RTs. Three years later production of the postwar version will begin and by 1954 the RT and its RTL and RTW relations will have established a monopoly in London, never achieved before or since, but for the time being the 151 members of the class are unique and the shape of things to come: they never quite supplanted my affection for the STL.

And today? Poor Malcolm, after passing the 11 plus, went to Dulwich College, worked for Wills cigarettes and died young of skin cancer, contracted during his visits to the tobacco plantations in the West Indies. Ironically both his parents, who might well not have survived the war, did. His Father became a teacher and they eventually retired to Somerset.

A number of STLs escaped breaking up, the best-known probably being the sit-up-and-beg STL469, often on display at the London Transport Museum in Covent Garden. Inevitably my favourites are the two roof numberbox versions, STLs 2093 and 2377, both in the safe keeping of the London Bus Preservation Group at Cobham.

The 159 is also still with us. It has been truncated – sorry about the elephant pun – and no longer reaches either the Zoo or Green Lane, but it continues to operate through the heart of the West End, from Oxford Circus to Streatham. Whilst virtually all the rest of the world has succumbed to OMO, London Transport remains faithful to conductors and open rear platforms for many of its most prestigious routes and the 159 is worked from Brixton Garage – once Telford Avenue tram depot – by a mixture of RMLs and a dedicated fleet of especially painted RMs in red and cream livery, the oldest of which entered service way back in 1959, only five years after the last STLs had ceased work in the streets of London. ■

CLASSIC BUS ALPHABET

Back by popular request. The CB ABC. Contributions by GAVIN BOOTH, STEWART J BROWN, ALAN MILLAR and STEPHEN MORRIS

A IS FOR ATLANTEAN. It's probably sacrilege to suggest that anything with the engine at the back could be considered a 'classic'. But it's now some 40 years since the Leyland Atlantean first appeared, turning the bus industry back to front. At first there was little advantage, other than an increase in passenger capacity to 78 and the ability of the driver to supervise loading; not until 1966 could you dispense with the conductor. Thereafter the Atlantean came into its own, and only very recently have manufacturers started to challenge its space-saving transverse engine arrangement. Towards the end of its very long production run the Atlantean came good, but in its early days it was an engineer's nightmare. But fashion won the day, the Atlantean, along with its rival Daimler Fleetline, saw off all the real classic designs and went on to be Britain's best-selling double-decker.

B IS FOR BUS-SPOTTER. In 1954 it would have cost you a shilling (5p) to join the Ian Allan Bus-Spotters Club. The Club rule was: 'Members of the Bus-spotters club will not in any way interfere with the working or material of any transport concern, nor be a nuisance to their staff, nor above all, trespass on their property. No one will be admitted to membership of the Club unless he solemnly promises to keep this rule'. Solemnly – phew! I never joined the Club – though I was in the parallel and infinitely more successful Locospotters Club – but that didn't stop me being terrified to set foot in bus garages in case the mighty hand of Ian Allan descended on my shoulder. For your shilling you got either a green or a red badge. If you wanted both badges you had to send 1s 6d (7 ½p). Oh yes – *and* a stamped addressed envelope.

C IS FOR CAUGHT BY THE CAMERA and other cliches beloved of caption writers in bus books and magazines. Rarely just photographed or snapped, buses and coaches are caught by the camera (caught in the act of what?), but as far as we're aware they're never nobbled by the notebook, trapped on tape or vacuumed by the video. Another favourite overworked and frequently misused word is 'resplendent'. Our dictionary tells us it's an adjective meaning brilliant, dazzingly or gloriously bright – a condition few buses remain in for more

Ian Allan **BUS-SPOTTERS CLUB**

Membership Application Form

RULE : Members of the Bus-spotters Club will not in any way interfere with the working or material of any transport concern, nor be a nuisance to their staff, nor above all, trespass on their property. No one will be admitted to membership of the Club unless he solemnly promises to keep this rule.

I, the undersigned, do hereby make application to join the Ian Allan Bus-spotters Club, and undertake, on my honour, if this application is accepted, to keep the above rule ; I understand that if I break it in any way I cease to be a member, and forfeit the right to wear the badge and take part in the Club's activities.

Date.............. 195... Signed...

These details should be completed in BLOCK LETTERS

Surname...
.... Date of Birth.........19......

Christian Names ....

Address ....
....
....

RED		GREEN	

Note : You can have EITHER a RED or GREEN badge for the enrolment fee of ONE SHILLING. If you want BOTH, the cost is 1/6.
Please mark your requirements with a cross (X).
I enclose Postal Order for.........s..........d.
IMPORTANT : A STAMPED, SELF-ADDRESSED ENVELOPE MUST BE ENCLOSED WITH YOUR APPLICATION AND REMITTANCE.

TEAR OFF HERE

than a day after they leave the paintshop, especially if they've genuinely just been caught by that ubiquitous camera. And while we're at it, don't forget how often a bus is said to have 'exemplified' a new livery, operator or type of vehicle or, indeed, how often a resplendent bus exemplifying the much loved identity of Universally Adored Motor Services/Road Car/Traction Company is 'seen here' or 'here seen' wherever it was caught by the camera when a simple word like 'at' or 'in' would do. Or is this paragraph just a classic case of 'c is for carp'?

D IS FOR DAIMLER. The Daimler name carried with it connotations of quality. Even royalty travelled in Daimlers, although the royal Daimlers tended to be limousines rather than CVD6s: about the same length, but with rather fewer seats and no conductor pressing you for your fare. And Daimler buses did seem to be a cut above the rest. The fluted top tank on exposed radiator models didn't need to carry a name badge in the way that chassis from other (lesser?) bus makers did. And that subtle anonymity perhaps said it all.

E IS FOR EXPERT. You'll see lots of these at bus rallies. It's not necessary to know much to be an expert, you just have to have a louder voice than anyone else and voice your opinion in such a way that no-one dare dispute it. Favourite line is: 'They were never like that in service'.

F IS FOR FARES. To paraphrase Dickens: running costs 99p, fares £1, result survival; running costs £1, fares 99p, result take-over by Stagecoach. On bus window notices the words 'Fares Revision' are industry-speak for 'Fares Increase'.

G IS FOR GARDNER, the diesel engine that became a legend in its own downtime. Designed for industrial and marine markets and first launched in 1928, Gardner's 4L2 was one of the first diesels (or 'oilers' as they were known then) to go into a British bus a couple of years later. By 1931, its LW range was in production for trucks and buses and the smaller 4LK followed four years later. Its reputation for slow revving, fuel economising reliability was well established and Gardner's total independence from chassis manufacturers made it popular across many makes. First choice in most Bristols, Guys, Daimlers, Atkinsons and Fodens, it went into often forgotten creations like GNR single-deckers in Ireland and half a dozen Gloster coaches built in 1933 for Red & White. Even AEC fitted Gardners in prewar Regals and Regents for Huddersfield and Hull and in Regent Vs for Aberdeen, Glasgow and Rochdale. Later still, Leyland installed it in Tigers and Nationals and other types we're not

Caught by the camera, a resplendent Daimler of 1910 exemplifying the early motor bus.

The engineer's dream: a Gardner 6LXB engine fitted to a London Transport Daimler Fleetline.

supposed to talk about in an unashamedly nostalgic publication like this. Like many legends, the Gardner's greatest beauty was in the eyes, ears and balance sheets of its beholders. It was good, but so were the in-house products of AEC, Leyland, Daimler and perhaps a few others. It's just that you rarely got them in another manufacturer's chassis.

H IS FOR HELL, HULL AND HALIFAX. These are the three famous Hs – Hell, Hull and Halifax. For those who've been to all three, Halifax is unquestionably the best even if considerably colder and wetter than the first on the list (but possibly not quite as cold as the middle one, which is just a bit too close to the icy North Sea to be comfortable). In the heyday of British buses Halifax's hills were climbed by hard-working AECs and Daimlers in a magnificent orange, green and cream livery, allegedly inspired by a demonstrator in Glasgow Corporation colours. It was ironic that while Glasgow abandoned these colours in 1959 (in the name of progress, let it be said), they lived on in Halifax until the creation of the West Yorkshire PTE in 1974.

And even without its orange, green and cream buses, Halifax is still a fine town.

I IS FOR INDEPENDENT. At one time 'Independent' meant any bus operator not in the public sector. Nowadays that means everyone except a few local authority operators like Lothian and Ipswich. But while at one time there were some very big independents, such as Lancashire United and West Riding, and there are always some very high-quality independents, Hedingham, Delaine and Epsom Coaches for example, the epitome of the independent operator was the little village bus company with a couple of Bedfords, three spanners and a dog. Its pet hates were 1) the big local operator, who was always held in the greatest contempt and 2) the men from the ministry, ditto. Restrictions like drivers' hours were a

Independent in a sea of publicly-owned buses. An AEC Reliance/Burlingham bus in the small fleet of Safeway of Guildford, an area dominated by London Transport and Aldershot & District.

nasty attempt to drive out the little man and were to be ignored, except where they applied to other bus companies. Of course, such operators never really existed, did they?

J IS FOR JJL. Developed by Marshall, adopted by General Motors, built by Bedford, abandoned by 1979 , well-regarded by many. The first attempt to build a rear-engined small bus, a pretty-looking 1976 package that anticipated the Dennis Dart of more than a decade later. Unfortunately it came too early: the UK bus industry wasn't yet ready for small buses. 'Son of JJL' appeared in 1995 as the Marshall Minibus; in fact it's a midibus, but who's counting?

K IS FOR KNOWLEDGE, something most of us possess in abundance in relation to buses and coaches – often in the most minute detail. While we may never have grasped the point of algebra, we can summon up the exact meanings of such alphanumeric codes as Crosville fleetnumbers or Leyland and AEC's chassis codes – like the difference between SLB290 and DLG802 or MU3RV and 2U3RA. We probably carry significant numbers to the grave because they were once worn by a bus we knew better than many more interesting people. Given a chance, we'll recite (hopefully just to ourselves when others aren't around to be bored) such useless knowledge as an entire city's bus route numbers and termini at some time in the past, but we'll forget to buy that urgently required loaf of bread or to remember an important family birthday. And our detailed knowledge of the history of an operator, vehicle or route will be out of all proportion to more useful skills like mastering a foreign language. But don't despair. It's harmless and no more eccentric (nor any less, either) than many other hobbies and pursuits and there are some useful by-products like the possession of a better developed sense of geography than others who've never felt the urge to find Chesterfield, Motherwell or Pontypridd on a map.

The young Thomas Knowles stands by the bus on which he was learning to drive in 1963, No L337. This Northern Counties-bodied Leyland PD2/1 was new in 1947 and is seen at Springfields. Note that no 'L' plates are carried as the trainee already held a car licence.

I SUPPOSE I was lucky, really, but to be brought up in the Potteries having been a wartime baby meant that I probably saw Potteries Motor Traction (PMT) at its best period. Gone were the days of the 1930s when the Potteries company had such poor profitability that the railway companies did not take a shareholding, as they did in most major bus companies. Gone were the days of wartime austerity, although some of those splendid utility Guys remained; instead the 1950s represented peak loadings and consolidation with the acquisition of many competitors, giving the fleet a variety that was probably unequalled throughout the land.

Unlike many enthusiasts, I always preferred PMT, the major operator in the area, to the independents, in spite of some of them operating very mixed and interesting fleets. PMT adopted a policy of retaining as many of the acquired vehicles as possible, but no petrol-engined machines were operated and to replace some of the more worn-out buses, visits were made to Frank Cowley the well-known and large secondhand bus dealer at Salford to purchase double-deckers to make up the fleet strength.

PMT entered the 1950s with an already varied fleet since during the War it had purchased its main competitor, the Associated Bus Companies Ltd which was an organisation made up of small operators who did not wish their activities to pass to PMT when they sold out. Nearly 30 vehicles from this fleet survived into the 1950s including some Leyland Tigers which were rebodied by Brush and Weymann just after the War. In addition to their indigenous prewar fleet of mainly Daimlers and Leylands (the last SOS having been withdrawn in 1949) there were the wartime Guys which mainly carried Strachan bodies, plus various oddments. The company set about postwar fleet renewal without any regard for standardisation. In 1945 three Roe-bodied Guys to relaxed utility specification arrived – the only Roe bodies to be bought new by PMT. Ten more Guys arrived in 1946 but these were fitted with Northern Counties bodies to highbridge specification – a brave move by PMT since the Potteries area is littered with low bridges which over the years have claimed several top decks – which is why these Guys spent most of their lives at Newcastle-under-Lyme garage. The same year saw the arrival of a dozen Brush-bodied AEC Regals whilst 1947 saw few new vehicles. However, an exchange of utility Bristols for the North Western Daimlers and Guys saw variety increased, whilst late in the year the first vehicles out of a batch of 25 lowbridge Northern Counties-bodied Leyland PD2/1s arrived, to be joined by a further 20 highbridge versions in 1949. Standardisation at last, I hear you say, but no – because 1948 saw a superbly smooth and reliable batch of ten Burlingham-bodied CVD6s arrive which were joined in 1949 by 11 similarly-bodied (except for being 8ft wide) Leyland OPS1/1s. These vehicles were powered by the wonderful prewar 8.6litre engine which meant that the tuneful note was still to be heard in North Staffordshire into the 1960s.

Eight 1936 PMT Leyland Tiger TS7s were given new Brush bodies in 1946 and three were transferred to the Wells Motor Services subsidiary in 1953/4. No S46 is seen in Stafford Street, Hanley in 1957, the year of its withdrawal.

All photos by Thomas W W Knowles

This picture was taken in Buxton Market Place where No SN126 was working as a duplicate on the joint service with North Western. A Leyland TS8 delivered new to PMT in 1938, the Burlingham body shown here was fitted in 1949.

No H207 joined PMT from City of Oxford in 1954 and is seen here in Newcastle bus station four years later. The Park Royal-bodied AEC Regent was new in 1940.

In spite of its registration, this Weymann-bodied Daimler COG5/40 was diverted to PMT in the early years of the War instead of being exported. After being re-engined, reregistered and rebuilt in the early 1950s No S218 survived until 1959. Alongside is H495, which was acquired with the small Davies fleet in 1954 – then fitted with a Hassall single-deck body.

This 1954 view shows L234, a Daimler CWG5 bodied by Brush which came to PMT from North Western in exchange for Bristol K5Gs during 1947.

Rebodying

At this time PMT decided to continue with its rebodying programme of prewar Leyland Tigers which started in 1946 with Brush. Bodies from Burlingham and Weymann were ordered along with 24 of the latter fitted on to Leyland OPD2/1 chassis in 1949/50. The story of these buses is worthy of an article of its own, but suffice to say here the bodies were removed a few years later for fitting to chassis acquired from independents, whilst double-deck bodies of three

kinds, all built by Northern Counties, were fitted to the chassis. Two of these rebodied vehicles survive today in preservation: L453 is owned by Nigel Parks who presents it in superb condition, whilst L466 is the flagship of the Potteries Omnibus Preservation Society which has recently undertaken much hard work on the bus.

Prior to the acquisition of a quantity of independents in the 1951-3 period, PMT took delivery of five Leyland-bodied Titans; a batch of Brush-bodied

PMT had many utility Guys rebodied by Northern Counties. The heavier examples like L248, seen at Stoke in 1959, were fitted in 1952.

Roe was an unusual body for the PMT fleet but the three Guy Arab II delivered in 1945 had lowbridge examples fitted. L279 is parked outside PMT's Tunstall enquiry office shortly before withdrawal in 1959.

Leyland PS2s; ten Windover coach bodies on prewar Tigers (and didn't the 8ft bodies on 7ft6in chassis make them sway!); ten Beadle coaches built using prewar Leyland units; the wartime Daimler COG5 single-deckers built for Salisbury, Southern Rhodesia, but diverted, were rebuilt and re-registered; whilst the superbly comfortable Burlingham-bodied Leyland Royal Tigers (with 'no' brakes) were on order.

With a variety like that, one would reasonably claim to be living in an area of outstanding interest. However, better was to come in that in 1951 no fewer than five companies were acquired, all of which operated in excess of 20 vehicles, many of which were retained. All except Mainwaring Bros. operated as subsidiary companies for some months. Mainwaring operated mainly to the west of Newcastle-under-Lyme to Audley (where its depot was), Butt Lane and Halmerend. It operated an unusual Sunday-only service from Audley to Alsager in Cheshire. All the prewar vehicles in this fleet were Leylands but postwar additions included Guys and Crossleys with the latter serving PMT until 1960. Within the fleet of two dozen were no fewer than 11 different bodybuilders!

In 1954 Northern Counties fitted new lightweight bodies to a number of Guys and Daimlers, like CWA6 No L286, acquired with the Browns business in 1952. Photographed in the winter snow of 1959, this bus survived until 1963 by which time it had received a red roof and upper deck window pillars.

Apart from a livery change, 1946 Northern Counties-bodied Guy Arab II No H293 looked just the same when photographed in Newcastle 13 years later. Note the PMT badge covering the Guy name on the radiator.

The prewar vehicles of the slightly larger Stoke on Trent Motors fleet were equally standardised except in this case all the vehicles had the same bodybuilder – Willowbrook. AECs and Leylands predominated along with an odd remaining Dennis Lancet I, whilst postwar additions, all of which operated for PMT for several years, included Guy, Leyland, AEC and Morris Commercial. In fact the company's two Lawton-bodied AEC Regal IIIs became the last halfcab single-deckers to operate for PMT when withdrawn in 1963. The company operated services in all the five (six including Fenton) towns and out to Barlaston, Meir, Milton and Bradwell. The Stoke to Milton road was shared with Milton Bus Service which had by far the most modern fleet taken over with just three prewar Leylands and 14 postwar examples supplemented by seven Guy Arab IIIs. This was the only fleet not to operate double-

deckers but once again variety was provided with bodies built by Willowbrook, Burlingham, Santus, SEAS, Pochin, Massey, Brush, Barnard and Metalcraft. As with the variety in the Mainwaring fleet many of the early postwar buses were built with unseasoned wood and were rebodied using the Weymann bodies from the OPD2/1s. Milton had a well-earned reputation for excellent timekeeping on its services to Abbey Hulton, Milton, Ball Green and it also reached Leek.

Thomas Tilstone & Sons ran an extensive network reaching Sandbach in the north, serving all the Potteries towns and Newcastle as well as operating to the new development at Blurton and the more established Chesterton, Red Street and Talke area. Four double-deckers were operated: a Willowbrook-bodied Leyland TD5 which boasted two gangways on the upper deck, two wartime Bristols and a Strachan-bodied AEC Regent III which was a regular performer with PMT on the Tunstall-Trentham route. My frequent use of this service made me well aware of its deep front dome which restricted vision from the front upstairs seats! All the prewar saloons were Leyland whilst the postwar fleet contained Leylands and AECs including an unusual pair of coaches bodied by Lawton and Strachan.

The last of the 'big five' was Browns (Tunstall) Ltd. Its premises were on the site of PMT's current Burslem garage from where they were operating about 40 vehicles at takeover. Browns operated mainly in the north of the Potteries, with services reaching Leek,

By the time this ex-Milton Bus Service Burlingham-bodied Guy Arab III, No S301, was photographed behind Newcastle depot in 1959, it had been withdrawn.

One of the very last all-red postwar vehicles to operate was Brush-bodied AEC Regal No S313, seen in the old wartime-built Longton bus station in 1958.

Sandbach, Alsager/Radway Green and they operated into Newcastle from the north. The fleet composition was quite different from that of the other acquired companies in that no vehicles had been delivered to Browns since 1946. However, the fleet contained ten Daimler CWA6s, most of which PMT had rebodied by NCME in 1954, and no fewer than 18 Bedford OWBs which were ousted immediately. Apart from an unfrozen Leyland TSII, the rest of the fleet comprised prewar AECs.

Secondhand buses

PMT was faced with a massive problem, and the way it tackled it created great interest for the enthusiast whilst at the same time rationalising its operations. To replace the unsuitable acquired vehicles, the company decided to purchase large numbers of secondhand AEC and Leyland diesel double-deckers. That was the limit of the standardisation and even then there were four Guy Arab IIs which had formed part of Hebble's fleet. Most of the vehicles were purchased from Frank Cowley who, I understand, made many trips to the Potteries with vehicles that were rejected. However, of the vehicles that were retained, some lasted with PMT for five years in spite of 134 new buses and coaches arriving between 1954 and 1956 so it was not until the

One of the Weymann bodies received on Leyland OPD2/1 Titans in 1949/50 was fitted to No S362, an ex-Tilstone Leyland PS1/1 Tiger, having been lengthened to 30ft. This 1960 picture shows a new-style destination blind incorporating the revised route-numbering system.

The acquisition of the Mainwaring business in 1951 brought this 1948 Barnard-bodied Leyland PS1/1 into the PMT fleet. When seen in Stafford Street, Hanley, in 1958, No SN370 was clearly feeling the cold!

1957 deliveries that PMT's prewar vehicles were more or less eliminated.

The secondhand vehicles acquired in this period included Leyland TD1s from Hants & Dorset and Wilts & Dorset; TD2s from Southdown; TD3s and TD4s from Hants & Dorset; with TD5s arriving from Ribble. The AEC Regents came from Oxford (with more in 1954), Glasgow and Halifax. During spring 1952, vehicles were also hired from Crosville and Leicester. The strains on the company were reflected in its 1953 deliveries which included ten Weymann-bodied Guy Arab IVs, diverted from Northern

General and 12 Northern Counties-bodied AEC Regent IIIs which allegedly were ordered by some of the acquired operators. Also delivered was a remarkable lightweight Daimler CLG5 with a Metro-Cammell body that was the forerunner of the Orion. This bus gained fame when new by being photographed by the media with its whole weight being supported by standing on six china tea cups!

Other measures were being taken by PMT at this time and these included a total service revision in the Potteries and Newcastle areas that enabled the acquired routes to be integrated with PMT's existing

Smooth running was the feature of the 10 Burlingham-bodied Daimler CVD6s delivered new to PMT in 1948. This view of No SN375 was taken at Longton bus station in the 1960 snow.

Below:
Photographed at the end of its life with PMT in 1960, Strachan-bodied AEC Regal III No C413 was new to Tilstones in 1948.

network. The result of this was the creation of longer linked services throughout, extending beyond the traditional 'Main Line' and giving a three-minute headway between each of the neighbouring six towns with excellent links from all the towns to Newcastle where Tunstall had the worst service, operating jointly with C M Dawson every 15 minutes off-peak and every ten minutes at peak. Another change that took place at the time was the elimination of the cream band from the red livery whilst in 1953 the fleet was renumbered into a sequence that approximated to age with a prefix to denote the type of vehicle. Thus C was a coach, S a single-decker, SN a saloon, H an highbridge and L a lowbridge double-decker. WN 4880 had the honour of becoming fleet No L1 having come from Brown's fleet. New to South Wales Transport in 1932, this AEC Regent had acquired an East Lancs lowbridge body.

By this time I had become very interested in PMT and just to add icing to the cake another operator was acquired in 1953 – Wells Motor Services of Biddulph. This company operated as a subsidiary until 1958 when the services were divided with North Western Road Car. The problem was that the routes operated straddled the boundaries set up by the area

Parked up in Hanley in 1961 is ex-Stoke Motors AEC Regal III No SN415 with locally-built Lawton bodywork. There were two such vehicles which had outlived all the other halfcab single-deckers when withdrawn in 1963.

This is the bus with poor forward visibility upstairs. Strachan-bodied AEC Regent III No L416 which was new to Tilstones is seen in Longton bus station in 1960. By this time it was wearing its third style of PMT livery.

agreements, since in addition to running into Tunstall and Hanley the company ran routes in South Cheshire around Congleton and even into Crewe on certain days of the week. A further most unusual long route into Crosville territory, which PMT retained, ran daily from Hanley through the North Potteries to Sandbach, Middlewich and Winsford to Over. This acquisition brought with it a number of Dennis Lancets of varying vintage but eventually we had the excitement of seeing PMT transfer some rebodied prewar Leylands to the Wells fleet which then received their green and cream livery.

Yes, the Potteries were certainly at their best in the 1950s, and PMT used the decade to consolidate its operations for the future. It was unfortunate that my photography did not really start until the late 1950s, but my interest gained from this era meant that when the time came to start work in 1960, it had to be at PMT. ■

THIS IS the antidote to CB's 'Classic Blunderbus' feature, proof I can write positively about Britain's bus building heritage, even if any random gathering of operators, engineers or drivers will likely damn the reputation of whole swathes of the postwar output of our chassis and body factories.

The object of this paeon of barely restrained praise is my nomination for the accolade of being the ultimate development of the front-engined halfcab double-decker – the Bristol Lodekka. The Routemaster may have it for refinement, longevity and novel construction, but it didn't do much that its predecessors couldn't do already and it didn't sell in anything like the same numbers as the Bristol. I'm sorry if you're a fan of all things Southall, but in my judgment and for all its relative crudeness, the Lodekka is the cleverer machine.

It gets there because it was the first practical lowheight double-decker with conventional seating layouts on both decks, but its triumph is all the more remarkable because Bristol got it right first time and set a standard others struggled to match.

Its appearance in 1949 signalled the imminent end of the side-gangway lowbridge 'decker that made life uncomfortable and inconvenient for passengers and conductors – an end hastened by the sheer simplicity of the new design.

Between them, Bristol and Eastern Coach Works stripped unnecessary height out of the bottom of an otherwise conventional bus, partly by going for semi-integral construction in which the chassis frame relied on the body for part of its strength. But the really clever bit was to design a back axle with a lower centre section and to divert the propeller shaft away from the centre of the bus, so the lower deck floor could be much nearer the ground.

The revolution stopped there and the rest of the Lodekka was refreshingly conventional. The prototypes had the same 8.1-litre AVW engine as Bristol built for its K-series 'decker, the constant mesh crash gearbox was hardly revolutionary and the optional Gardner 5LW and 6LW engines were equally familiar. That suited the Tilling and Scottish Bus Group companies which, thanks to the terms of

CLASSIC WONDER BUS

ALAN MILLAR changes direction and hails an all-time great bus

Below: **The lower saloon of the 1949 Lodekka prototype. Production examples had a neater floor arrangement, but for nearly half-a-century ago, it represented a significant advance.**

Bottom: **The 1949 prototype Lodekka in the Bristol Tramways fleet, showing the broad radiator that only featured on the two early prototypes. All subsequent Lodekkas had full-width 'new look' fronts.**

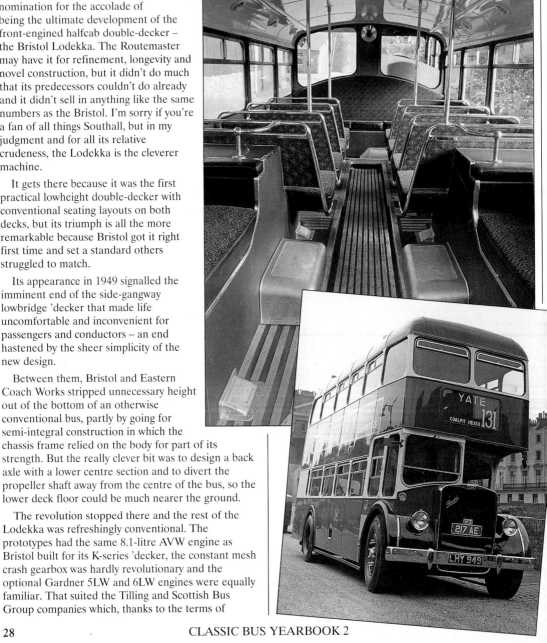

nationalisation, were to be its only customers.

To say the designers didn't even waste their initial efforts on styling is to be kind. The first prototype's squashed and butchered K-type body and massive exposed radiator made it little short of ugly, but the second was a definite improvement and the even better proportioned, concealed radiator production models made up for the earlier concentration on getting the business end to work properly.

What followed was steady evolution: BVW, 6LX and Leyland O.600 engines, air suspension at the back, flat floors instead of a sunken lower deck centre gangway, forward entrances, 30ft and 31ft versions and latterly even semi-automatic gearboxes.

By the end of production in 1968, the Lodekka's 5,217 sales put the Routemaster's 2,875 in the shade and rivals struggled to sell 900 lowheight halfcabs between them. The original LD accounted for 2,181, there were seven 30ft LDL and nine 27ft LDSs, followed by 1,867 FLFs, 890 FSs, 218 FSFs and 45 FLs; 1,105 went to Scottish companies, the rest to ex-Tilling, Red & White and Balfour Beatty fleets in England and Wales. By the mid-1960s there were Lodekkas from Inverness to Land's End.

The popular FLF was built for Tilling and Scottish Bus Group fleets. This Bristol Omnibus FLF found itself in the former independent West Riding fleet after it was taken over by the Transport Holding Company.

M Fowler

The FSF was one of the rarer Lodekka variants. This 1962 FSF6G was new to Central SMT and was still wearing Central red livery when first sold to Eastern Scottish, as seen here in Edinburgh in 1977.

Alan Millar

Its success was helped by a neat design which lacked some of its rivals' awkward compromises. Sure, it was a squeeze in places and rear-entrance versions were generally neater than FLFs and FSFs, but it never seemed bodged and that made it a perfectly acceptable substitute for highbridge buses in several fleets.

Had it been available on the open market, life would have been different. No Dennis Loline certainly, for who would have needed a licence-built Lodekka? Maybe no AEC Bridgemaster either. But the Lodekka might have gained such refinements as a semi-automatic gearbox a lot more quickly had large municipals been able to buy it.

There could even have been a less low Lodekka, for if the original design squeezed acceptable headroom into a 13ft 6in 'decker, a 14ft version could have combined the interior accommodation of a highbridge

bus with a lower centre of gravity and less risk of bridge and tree damage.

Bristol seems to have thought so too and announced the separate-chassised LDL (no relation to the 1958 prototypes with the same code) when it returned to the open market in 1965. But it was too late. What might have been a winner 10 years earlier was doomed to stay on the drawing board as the market deserted half cabs for rear engines.

But don't write the Lodekka off as a 1950s throwback. Forget the crash gearbox which was a requirement of its conservative customers. And forget its eventual unsuitability for one-person operation; that's an irrelevance – judging yesterday's bus by today's standards.

It took front-engined half cabs to new limits of versatility – and it worked. For that alone it's one of the great milestones of 20th century bus design. Nothing less. ∎

SCOTLAND
1939

In the last long summer of peace, R D OKILL visited Scotland with his camera

On private hire work, this 1937 Leyland Tiger TS7 with Burlingham 33-seat full-fronted coach body was in the sizeable fleet of Greenock Motor Services, a Western SMT subsidiary. This bus passed to Western when the GMS services were absorbed in 1949 and was withdrawn in 1957.

A splendid 1938 Albion Valkyrie PW145 with Cowieson bodywork in the famous fleet of Young's of Paisley. Note how the Albion sunrise logo is echoed on the radiator grille.

At Luss, on Loch Lomondside, a Central SMT Leyland Tiger TS4 with Pickering 32-seat rear entrance bus body, one of a batch of 50 delivered in 1932. It was withdrawn in 1949.

Built in 1934 for the Alexanders associate, General Motor Carrying Co of Kirkcaldy, this 1934 Leyland Lion LT5B had Alexander 32-seat bus bodywork. GMC was absorbed into the main Alexanders fleet in 1937, and this bus continued to work in the Fife area until 1955. Although it was a Leyland Lion, it had a Leyland 8.6 litre engine and was numbered in the P (Tiger) series.

Alexanders built up a massive fleet of Leyland Tigers in the prewar years. No P252 was one of 52 1935 TS7s with Alexander 32-seat coach bodywork and is seen here on the Glasgow-St Andrews service. All but one were rebuilt to Titan TD4 specification and rebodied as double-deckers in 1943/4, and some survived until 1961 in this form.

A later Alexanders Tiger, a TS8 with Alexander 35-seat coach body, one of 50 bought in 1939. This bus was still in the fleet when the Alexanders empire was split into three in 1961, although it was withdrawn the following year. Alongside is a Duple-bodied Bedford WTB from the fleet of Campbells of Whitburn.

Most of Alexanders Leyland Tigers in the mid-late 1930s had coach-style seating, but a batch of unashamed buses was bought in 1937. These were TS7s with Alexander 32-seat bodies and in this view of the first of the batch can be seen the roof luggage rack and the steps leading to it.

Following page: An amazing prewar colour view of Alexanders R37, a 1932 Leyland Titan TD2 with Leyland lowbridge 48-seat bodywork, seen *en route* for Alloa in the Hillfoots towns. It was one of 25 similar buses bought that year, and by 1935 had received a Leyland 8.6 litre diesel engine in place of its original petrol unit. Alexanders, like other companies in the SMT group, was an early convert to the idea of diesel engines. The bus was withdrawn in 1950.

THE DECLINE AND FALL OF THE Leyland EMPIRE

GAVIN BOOTH celebrates the 1996 centenary of Leyland's first vehicles by admitting – reluctantly – that Leyland didn't always get it right.

Heralding a brave new era: one of the prototype Atlanteans at the 1958 Earls Court Commercial Motor Show. With Weymann semi-lowbridge body, it was the first of a number for BET fleet James of Ammanford. Unfortunately the early Atlanteans did not always perform reliably, and it was the 1972-introduced AN68 that restored the Atlantean's reputation.

IT'S 1963. Imagine what Donald Stokes, at the head of the newly-formed Leyland Motor Corporation, must have been thinking. Here was Leyland in an apparently unassailable position – sales were booming, even export business was good, the model range was the most comprehensive offered by a UK-based bus and truck builder – and the company had started expanding into the volume car business at a time when private motoring was really taking off. To cap it all, you had taken over – sorry, 'merged with' – your most tenacious competitor. What could possibly go wrong?

End of an ERA? Ten 1938 all-Leyland lowbridge Titan TD5cs proudly lined up in Chesterfield Corporation's garage. This was Leyland as many people still prefer to remember it.

What indeed?

The answer, as we now know, is just about everything. Poor old Leyland became the butt of music-hall jokes as it struggled to cope with its troubled car businesses, while at the same time it seemed to be ignoring its long-standing bus and truck business. Add to that nationalisation and privatisation – one might say Thatcherisation – and more recently Volvo-isation, and it is clear that Leyland's failure to reach its century as a manufacturer this year is the result of misfortune, mismanagement, misreading of the markets, and probably quite a few other mis-prefixed words as well.

Among Leyland fans – and here the writer is proud to stand up and be counted – the rot really started after Leyland set out on the acquisition trail in the 1960s. Before that Leyland Motors Ltd had been a substantial and successful business, selling buses and trucks throughout the world. Not just any buses, though. There had been dozens of firms in Britain in the 1920s and 1930s building bus and coach chassis, with varying degrees of success. Although Leyland had been building buses since 1900, its breakthrough really came with the Titan TD1 double-deck model in 1927, and a succession of ever-better Titans and Tigers, as well as Lions, Cheetahs, Cubs and other big cats, followed until, at the outbreak of World War 2 in 1939, Leyland was vying with AEC for top billing.

AEC had a vital ingredient: London custom. Its historical links with the London General company put it in a strong position as principal chassis supplier to the 1933-created London Passenger Transport Board. Leyland managed to get a foot in the (doubtless elegantly-designed) London Transport door, but mainly building small batches of smaller-size and advanced-design models. AEC had the volume business with its Regent and Regal models and this undoubtedly worked to AEC's competitive advantage.

Opposite directions

After the War AEC and Leyland developments seemed to happen in parallel. There were big-engined double-deckers, underfloor-engined single-deckers, lightweight underfloor-engined single-deckers, longer double-deckers. But at this point AEC and Leyland moved in opposite directions. AEC had dabbled with the underfloor-engined Regent IV double-decker and later the integral lowheight Bridgemaster while Leyland pursued the rear-engine layout, culminating in the still-familiar Atlantean.

So, back to 1963. Donald Stokes would surely have felt a warm glow as he read Derek Moses' municipal bus fleet analysis in *The Commercial Motor*. Leyland was a clear leader with 7,166 buses in service with the

Some operators continued to buy Leyland Titans with exposed radiators even when 'new-look' fronts were on offer. This Manchester Corporation PD2/34 of 1958 is seen after transfer to the Selnec PTE fleet, looking slightly incongruous in the modern orange/cream colours.

Gavin Booth

UK's corporation and urban district council fleets. That figure was nearly 6% up on the previous years and represented four in every ten municipal motorbuses. Its nearest rivals were way behind: Daimler (4,210), AEC (3,625) and Guy (1,558). Away from the municipalities, Leyland and AEC had an equally strong hold on the British Electric Traction (BET) group companies, and while Leyland would continue as major supplier to the Scottish Bus Group fleets right to the end of SBG, AEC's popularity in Scotland was waning. The nationalised Tilling fleets were still tied into the Bristol/Eastern Coach Works combination for all but a handful of their vehicle intake.

London Transport was different, of course. Heavily AEC-dominated, with Leyland a relatively small player, LTE in 1963 was in the midst of its Routemaster programme, to be followed by unhappy forays into other makes.

A glance at the Leyland 1963 model list was also a cause for quiet confidence. The single-deckers started with the lightweight Comet, by now an export model, and then there was the lightweight underfloor-engined Tiger Cub, the heavier Leopard, and the export models – the Royal Tiger Worldmaster, Olympic and Tiger. The faithful Titan was still the double-deck mainstay, but the new rear-engined Atlantean was increasingly winning orders, and there was the

lowheight Lowlander, built by Albion but sold as a Leyland outside Scotland.

So – no worries then? Not a bit of it.

Leyland's previous acquisitions had been straightforward, adding specialist manufacturers to the group – Albion, Scammell, Self-Changing Gears; but the purchase of the Standard-Triumph car company in 1961 took Leyland into new and unfamiliar areas. Soon after that came the 'merger' with arch-rival AEC, and it was soon clear that power was to be concentrated in the small town of Leyland, Lancashire.

The first fruits of Leyland's new links with AEC were the Leyland Panther and AEC Swift chassis, rushed into production to cater for a perceived demand for rear-engined single-deck citybus chassis. Although neither was a failure in sales terms, they were nowhere near as popular as their underfloor-engined contemporaries, the Leyland Leopard and AEC Reliance, even though the Swift was the favoured

chassis for London Transport's misguided move to high-capacity single-deckers in the mid-1960s.

Growth strategy

Faced with the prospect of increasing competition at home and overseas from its rapidly-expanding rivals in mainland Europe, Leyland embarked on a growth strategy which in the course of the 1960s took Leyland Motors

from being a well-regarded Lancashire-based specialist builder to being the British Leyland Motor Corporation (BLMC), the major force in the UK motor industry. First there was a share exchange with the Transport Holding Company which gave Leyland a 25% stake in Bristol and Eastern Coach Works (ECW) and allowed Bristol/ECW products on to the open market for the first time in over 15 years.

That was peanuts, though. In 1967 came Rover/Alvis, and in 1968 Leyland mopped up virtually the rest of the UK-owned motor industry. British Motor Holdings (BMH) had been formed following the 1966 merger of British Motor Corporation (essentially Austin and Morris) with Jaguar Cars

(Jaguar, Daimler and Guy). BMH was not a happy firm, and by 1968 it was dying on its feet. The sale of the ailing BMH was politically-inspired, but it appeared to fit in with BLMC's expansionist plans.

Unfortunately the volume car business was in a mess; Austin/Morris models were technically advanced but poorly made and marketed. But at least the merger brought old enemies like Daimler and Guy into Leyland control. For much of the postwar period, certainly since 1950, the four main players in the UK bus market had been AEC, Daimler, Guy and Leyland. AEC had of course been part of the Leyland empire for the past six years, but control of Guy and, more significantly, Daimler, was a valuable prize.

Leyland Motors Ltd built this Titan PD2/10 for Gellygaer UDC in 1953. The Farington-style body – though preferably the highbridge version rather than the lowbridge one seen here – was probably the author's all-time favourite.

Export was an important part of Leyland's business, with chassis and complete buses being despatched to all points of the world in the 1940s and 1950s. These all-Leyland Farington-style Titans are loaded in a ship ready to sail for South Africa.

Models like the lightweight underfloor-engined Tiger Cub sold well to BET group customers. This 1957 example with Willowbrook 45-seat body went to Yorkshire Traction in Barnsley.

The Leopard competed hard with AEC's Reliance for coach business in the 1960s and 1970s. This 1964 36ft Leopard with Plaxton Panorama bodywork was one of many used by Ribble group fleet Standerwick for long-distance work. Note the carefully-posed 'passengers' in this official view.

As a force in bus manufacturing, Guy was clearly on the wane. A minor player before World War 2, its fortunes were boosted when it was chosen as one of the handful of suppliers of new double-deck buses during the War. Guy's reputation for indestructible reliability led many customers to continue buying Guys well into the postwar years, but the ill-conceived Wulfrunian model brought the company to its knees and it never recovered.

Daimler, on the other hand, was on a roll. Its main strength had been as a builder of double-deck buses for urban service, but its 1960-introduced Fleetline

broadened its customer base. Here was a rear-engined double-deck chassis to rival Leyland's Atlantean, and with the Gardner engine so loved by chief engineers. BET and SBG companies that had rarely looked at Daimlers before were suddenly queueing up to buy Fleetlines. But not Roadliners; Daimler's foray into rear-engined single-deckers was even less successful than Leyland's.

The UK bus-manufacturing industry had been caught wrong-footed with rear-engined single-deckers. When they were introduced, in the first half of the 1960s, double-deck one-person operation (opo) was

A brand-new West Yorkshire Road Car Leyland National in full NBC corporate 'glory' at Harrogate bus station in 1974. For some years this was the standard single-deck bus available to NBC fleets.

Gavin Booth

A shortage of Bristol VRTs turned NBC back to the Leyland Atlantean. This 'all-Leyland' product is an AN68/1R with an attractive two-door Park Royal body style evolved for NBC. It is seen when new on a private hire at Chessington Zoo in 1974.

Gavin Booth

not legal, and some influential operators were turning to large-capacity opo single-deckers instead of double-deckers. But then the rules changed: from July 1966 opo double-deckers were legalised, and by the end of the decade the double-decker was back with a vengeance.

Unease

For Leyland, this was fine. If you wanted a double-decker you had to buy from BLMC. End of story. You could have an Atlantean or a Fleetline or, from 1968, a Bristol VRT. But if it was fine for Leyland, it was less

so for Leyland's customers. There was unease about Leyland's monopoly and a feeling among operators that Leyland's eye was off the ball and the company was too busy trying to rescue its sick car business to worry about the buses.

And if that wasn't bad enough the whole bus industry was thrown into turmoil by the far-reaching effects of the 1968 Transport Act. This, among other things, set up the first Passenger Transport Executives (PTEs), created the National Bus Company (NBC), and introduced Bus Grants – initially 25% of the cost of a new bus, but set to grow to 50% – to encourage

operators to upgrade their fleets with buses suitable for opo.

Needless to say, Bus Grants encouraged a buying boom, and Leyland was the main beneficiary. Out went the front-engined double-deckers from AEC, Bristol, Daimler, Guy and Leyland, which didn't meet the Grant specification, and production of the rear-engined models moved up a notch. The improved Atlantean AN68 model came in 1972 and this restored the faith of many customers, but there was still a feeling that Leyland was paying no attention to its customers and was operating on a 'take it or leave it' basis.

That feeling was reinforced when the Leyland National was unveiled in 1970. This integral single-deck bus was the outcome of a partnership between Leyland and NBC and quickly sounded the death-knell

for the rear-engined single-deck chassis from AEC, Bristol, Daimler and Leyland.

What rivalry there was for Leyland's products had come from Bedford and Ford, operating at the lighter end of the market, and from Seddon and Metro-Scania. Seddon's Gardner-engined RU and the MCW/Scania collaboration competed with the National, but only really nibbled at the edges.

Then in 1973 Leyland's double-deck domination was threatened by two new models, the Scania-MCW Metropolitan, and the front-engined Ailsa, and while some operators expressed their feelings by ordering the new models, they never really damaged Leyland's position.

But Leyland wasn't taking any chances and worked to develop a new-generation double-decker that would replace its Atlantean/Fleetline/VRT range. This was

Above: **Ribble took one of the first of Leyland's rear-engined Panthers in 1964 and fitted a Marshall 49-seat express coach body to it. It was to be Ribble's only Panther.**

Below: **The Titan PD3s sold to Coras Iompair Eireann were given rather anachronistic CIE bodies based on Leyland's prewar body – note the triple upstairs front window and the seven-bay body construction. Leyland went on to supply Atlanteans to CIE, but lost out to a breed of locally-assembled buses in the 1980s. Leyland double-deckers returned to favour with the Olympian.**

the B15, later named Titan, which turned out to be more advanced than most customers really wanted, and over its troubled seven-year production life sold almost exclusively to London Transport. It was discontinued in 1984, the same year as the older, simpler and infinitely better-selling Atlantean.

While the buses could virtually sell themselves, sales of BLMC's cars were suffering from an outdated model range, and most of the company's profits were being ploughed into the car business – profits that were largely coming from the sales of buses and trucks.

With the rest of Britain, Leyland struggled through the dark days of the electricity cuts and the three-day week in 1973/4, which caused chassis and body orders to get seriously out of step, and it was some years before the bus delivery situation had settled down again. In the meantime, though, a Labour government

was elected in 1974, and BLMC was nationalised.

A start was made on sorting out the mass of commercial vehicle models and factories. The hallowed ground of AEC, Southall was closed in 1979, followed in 1980 by the Park Royal coachworks. These two sites had played a significant part in the development of the motorbus, and some of the most classic designs of all time rolled out of their gates. The Titan, which had been built at Park Royal, moved to the Leyland National plant at Workington, a taste of what was to come.

Operator resistance

Although the Titan had been intended as a replacement for the entire Leyland double-deck range, operator resistance forced the company to produce a new, simpler model, unveiled in 1980 as the Olympian.

Built initially at Bristol, the Olympian moved to Workington in 1983, then Farington, Leyland in 1986, and back to Workington in 1990.

The Olympian saw off the Fleetline (in 1980), VRT (1981) and Atlantean (1984).

Leyland had not been short of suitors over these years. Fiat/Iveco, Renault, Volvo and even MCW came to discuss mergers or collaborations, but nothing came of these discussions.

The Thatcher government had introduced competition into Britain's bus industry outside London, and was busy dismantling the state-owned NBC and SBG undertakings.

The range was changing, though. The Olympian was now the sole double-deck model, though having to compete hard with MCW's Metrobus. The National, in its revised National 2 form, was fading out, and in 1985 was replaced by the Lynx, supposedly to be offered with bodies from other manufacturers, but the standard model was a complete bus built at Workington. The trusty Leopard had given way to the Tiger in 1981, an overdue updating of the underfloor-engine formula, but while the Leyland found regular business from the public sector operators, Volvo's B10M had been introduced just a year earlier, and quickly became market leader. More surprising was the Royal Tiger, a rear-engined coach offered as an underframe or as a complete coach, the Doyen. In the smaller midi-size market, the rather basic Cub had been replaced by the Swift.

Sense of relief

But time was running out and Leyland needed more than new models. The government was keen to get British Leyland off its hands, and although MCW was among the interested parties, Leyland Bus went to its management in 1987 – but not for long, as things were to turn out. For many there was a sense of relief that Leyland hadn't passed into overseas control; its sister, Leyland Trucks, had been sold to DAF.

The new owners of Leyland Bus made encouraging noises about the future of the range, and for a short while it looked as if the company was back on the right track.

It was to be a very short while. The next year Leyland Bus was sold on to Volvo.

At first the two ranges were allowed to sell in parallel, but it was clear that something would have to give. The Tiger, outclassed by the B10M was an obvious casualty, and sure enough it was dropped. In the absence of a viable Volvo alternative, the Lynx seemed to have a future; Volvo had said as much when it took over. But the Lynx too was dropped, along with Volvo's slow-selling B10R, in favour of the new B10B.

The most obvious survivor was the Olympian, by a clear head the world's best-selling double-decker both in the UK and in three-axle form in the Far East markets. And the Olympian did survive, badged as a Leyland until 1993 when the sad closure of the Workington plant signalled the end of the Leyland name.

The Olympian survived the closure, though. Volvo recognised its value and relaunched it in a Volvo-ised

Leyland Titans and Nationals undergoing pre-delivery inspection at the Workington plant in 1981. The Titans are, almost inevitably, for London, the Nationals for West Yorkshire. The revised front of the National 2 compares with the 1974 West Yorkshire National seen on an earlier page.

Gavin Booth

version, with a choice of Cummins or Volvo engines. Even the Olympian name survives, unique in a range that is otherwise known only by model numbers. Speaking to Volvo it is clear that the company recognises the importance of its heritage, and in particular the many world-leading models that came out of that Lancashire factory.

But Volvo has little time for sentiment, and while there were many who were sorry to see the disappearance of the Leyland name, some felt that it had been devalued to an extent by a number of models that seemed to have been cobbled together in a hurry to meet a perceived market demand.

The last 30 years were not the happiest in Leyland's long history, but it wasn't all bad. There are Leopards, Tigers, Nationals, Lynxes, Atlanteans, Titans and Olympians that will be running in service for a long time as a reminder of Leyland's important legacy.

The bus manufacturing industry worldwide is moving towards a small number of specialists geared up to produce the relatively small quantities involved. Had Leyland's own ambition not got caught up with the politicking of the 1960s, 1970s and 1980s, it might well have survived to be one of that select few. ∎

WHEN DUPLE WAS DOMINANT, BUT PLAXTON WAS SUPREME

A bus by any other name might smell the same, suggests ALAN MILLAR

W HEN YOU recall the buses of your youth – the ones that sparked off the interest which has led you to buy (or have bought for you) this book you're reading today – and compare them with today's technically refined creations, do you wonder why you prefer the obsolescent and extinct to the seemingly bland?

Perhaps it's the personal memories of travelling to school, visiting now deceased but fondly remembered relatives or going on holiday. Or is it the quasi-Edwardian livery, the sweeping line, polished radiator, varnished woodwork, opulent moquette and soft lighting which is ever so slightly more Edwardian, better swept, more highly polished, varnished, opulent and soft in hindsight than it was on a wet winter's evening? Or again, is it a musical memory of a more primitive engine and gearbox whining and roaring away from a stop in a manner that the likes of a Dennis Dart will never begin to emulate?

Let me throw in another thought. Do we have a particular fondness for the buses of yesterday because most of them had names? I suspect that a tiny part of many enthusiasts' xenophobia is fuelled by multinational manufacturers' practice of identifying their products by numbers which convey information at the expense of character.

Take Mercedes-Benz, for example. Now, I don't consider myself at all xenophobic when it comes to people, countries or buses, I've got nothing against Mercedes' products and I fully understand that numbers cross linguistic frontiers more successfully than many words. But how can you get to grips with a regime in which midibuses with seemingly widely different designations of 709D and 814D have far more in common with each other than a high-specification coach and a humble citybus with adjacent designations of O404 and O405?

Descriptive names like Royal Tiger and Tiger Cub positioned their products more precisely in our minds and those of potential customers. Or so we think today.

Published histories suggest manufacturers didn't bother with model names before the mid-1920s. Presumably their production runs were so short and their potential markets so narrow that they could easily get away with simply describing them by their companies' names or with functional descriptions like 'four-tonner', 'two-axle' or '40hp'.

The *Regent* was one of AEC's longest-surviving names – it was in use for nearly 40 years. This was a late-model Regent III, a 1956 Ipswich Corporation bus with Park Royal 56-seat body.

Gavin Booth

A rare Leyland name-badge, for the 1960s export rear-engined single-deck *Lion*.

But as their buses became more durable and their potential markets grew in size, sophistication and susceptibility to the blandishments of advertising copy, they identified their models more clearly and tantalisingly, starting with letters and/or numbers.

Some, like Daimler, Bristol and Bedford, named few models and hardly suffered for it, even if Bedford's VAS, VAM and VAL are usually spoken of as if they were words rather than initials – while I've never heard anyone ever call an OB an 'Obb'. And the urge to use names leads at least some East Anglians to refer to Bristol FLFs (part of Bristol's only named model range) as 'Fluffs'.

Twelfth letter

Back in 1925, Leyland and AEC were among the first to use names. Leyland alliterated – matching its own name with models called Leviathan, Lion, Lioness, Leopard and Leveret – but its imaginative use of the 12th letter of the alphabet was immediately exhausted and within two years it was developing new name themes from those originals.

So the Leviathan (a Biblical sea monster) started a policy of giving all but one of Leyland's subsequent double-deckers a giant-sounding name ending in 'an'. Greek mythology brought Titan (a race of giants) from 1927 until 1968 and again from 1977 to 1984, Atlantean from 1956 and Olympian from 1980.

Atlantean was the only adjective. For, contrary to popular misconception, it doesn't commemorate someone born aboard ship in mid-Atlantic but comes from a Latin word, Atlanteus, describing someone with the strength of the giant Atlas who was made to hold up the pillars separating heaven and earth as punishment for his part in the revolt of the Titans against the Olympians – hence Atlas holding the globe on earlier Atlantean badges.

The Olympians were descendants of a particularly superior and magnificent Greek god, but Leyland had upset its sequence with a 1953-8 Olympian which was neither superior, magnificent nor double-deck. It sold about about 56 of this Metro-Cammell Weymann-bodied integral lightweight, so named because it complemented the heavier Olympic launched four years earlier and because Olympic Cub would have sounded stupid.

The Olympic sold well, but had to be rechristened Levend in Istanbul after a national military hero, to avoid insulting Turkish pride with a name from arch-enemy Greece. Olympic also happened to be the name of a rather fine White Star liner that plied the North Atlantic from 1911 to 1935, a fact of barely passing consequence had Leyland not given its only non-'an'-ending double-decker the same name as the Olympic's more famous sister ship.

That sister ship was the Titanic which was at least as fine a ship, but only plied the North Atlantic for four days in April 1912 before colliding with an iceberg, plunging to the bottom of the ocean with two-thirds of its passengers and crew and becoming history's most famous shipwreck.

Barely 15 years later, Leyland's six-wheel Titan was christened Titanic, probably only because the word means huge or colossal. Yet Titania, Titian or Titan Six would have been a more tasteful choice which could hardly have given it a less disastrous commercial performance as Leyland only sold 47 Titanics. Alan Townsin, to whose encyclopaedic knowledge I will bow in most matters, suggests the name may have been a black joke on the part of Leyland's chief engineer, G J Rackham, who saw no future in six-wheel 'deckers.

Titan was an altogether more inspired choice, best remembered by Leyland's classic call for municipal transport managers to 'Buy a Titan and bury a tram'. In 1932, a mere pretender in the market, Gilford, called its new double-decker the Zeus after the Greek god of sky and weather who defeated the Titans and Olympian deities. Two sales hardly made this Zeus a match for the Titan and it was the Gilford deity that disappeared in 1936. Its Hera single-decker (named after Zeus's wife and sister – the only name to acknowledge the sometimes incestuous nature of the bus industry?) fared only marginally better.

For its mainsteam single-deckers, Leyland took up the wild cat theme of its Lion and Leopard, starting

Named after 'a virtually unpronounceable antelope', one of Leyland's 1939 twin-steer *Gnus*. This coach, for City of Brentwood, has Duple bodywork.

Looking suitably *Regent* in Eastbourne Corporation's cream/blue livery, an AEC MkV of that type with East Lancs bodywork. Even the destinations have royal connections . . .

with the Tiger and bonneted Tigress. Two sales rendered the original Leopard a bigger flop than the Titanic, but the underfloor engined Leopard of 1959 was one of Leyland's greatest successes.

That's one of the things about model names. Manufacturers go to expensive lengths to register and protect them, even to register and protect names they don't want rivals to use, so their options for new names are limited and it makes sense to recycle them at respectable intervals. Lion resurfaced three times postwar, first on an unsuccessful rear-engined export single-decker in the sixties, then occasionally and somewhat half-heartedly on some B21 export chassis in the seventies and finally on 32 underfloor-engined double-deckers imported in the mid-1980s from DAB in Denmark.

The name *Swift* was used on AEC's rear-engined bus chassis. This 1971 London Country Swift, seen in Stevenage SuperBus livery, has a Metro-Cammell body. The Swift name was revived by Leyland in the 1980s.
Gavin Booth

Plaxton and Duple vied to be number one builder of coach bodies, and this was reflected in their model names. This 1973 Bristol RELH6L from the Greenslades fleet, seen touring in Bowness in National Express livery, has a 46-seat Plaxton *Panorama Elite* body.
Gavin Booth

Tiger was recycled more successfully as Royal Tiger (twice), Tiger Cub (also twice), Royal Tiger Cub and in its own right on the Leopard's successor in 1981. Cub, for Leyland's smaller cats, was first used in 1931, before being used as a diminutive suffix on various shorter or lighter versions of postwar single-deckers, and resurfaced again in 1979 on its own as a truck-derived midibus.

There were three other cats. Cheetah, named after the fastest mammal on earth, was a 1935-40 lightweight cross between the Lion and Cub of its day; the name nearly made a comeback in the 1980s when Leyland considered relaunching the Bristol LHS midicoach. The cat cheetah is a member of the leopard family, as is the panther, so it was fitting that Leyland's 1964 rear-engined single-decker was called the Panther (and its shorter version Panther Cub) as its closest relative in the range was the mid-engined Leopard.

It took far longer for the third cat to make it as a mainstream bus. In a moment of apparent aberration, Leyland used the alliterative Lynx for a truck version of the Cheetah and revived it on a 1960s truck. A few of both were exported as buses, but it wasn't until 1985 that a real Lynx bus was produced.

Duple chose the name *Dominant* for its 1970s coach range. This 1981 Dominant II on Leyland *Leopard* at Heathrow Airport is a London Country vehicle in Green Line Jetlink 747 livery.
Gavin Booth

Bristol moved away from its normal model letters to call its 1949 lowfloor double-decker the *Lodekka* – surely an inspired name. This 1966 York-West Yorkshire Lodekka, seen against a backdrop of York Minster and the City Walls, is an FS6B example. Like all Lodekkas it has an Eastern Coach Works body.
Gavin Booth

Leyland – and, following the inevitable exchange of lawyers' letters, settled for Alternative Chassis Engineering. That helped assuage any grudge still borne on behalf of the real AEC for having had to call itself ACLO in South American markets where the German AEG company's trademark was already established.

Warships

AEC first named its buses after warships. Blenheim, Grenville and Ramillies (the latter a victorious battle against France in the War of the Spanish Succession) fortunately didn't stick, but Renown did and encouraged AEC to pursue an 'R' theme instead with Regent, Regal, Reliance and Ranger – all five names recycled across various models in subsequent decades. There even was a Leyland-badged Ranger for export in the 1980s.

Albion pursued a similar policy with 'V' names – starting (and finishing) with Viking and adding Valkyrie (after mythical Teutonic maidens who carried slain warriors off to Valhalla), Valiant, Victor, Valorous and Venturer. After the last Venturer double-decker was built in 1951, Plaxton took up the name for one of its coach bodies and it made another comeback in the mid-1980s when, for the only time in its history, Bedford named a model – its 12 metre YNV – in a belated attempt to restore its days of past glory.

The leporine theme of the Leveret wasn't pursued, but Leyland's zoo (which also included such trucks as the Bull, Beaver and Hippo) included eight Gnus (after a virtually unpronounceable antelope) and one Panda. By the 1980s, its lawyers probably wished it had registered Puma and Cougar, for those cat names were used audaciously by the new ACE company for its hand-built chassis. ACE had less success in calling itself AEC (for Albion Equipment Company) – stealing the names of two businesses acquired by

All these manufacturers' naming policies reveal virtues others tried to emphasise in the way they

advertised their products – the power of wild animals, legendary strength, military or regal potency or plain and simple endurance. Having got there first, Leyland, AEC and Albion left others to try and fill the gaps with varying degrees of success and taste.

Guy used mammals for its small buses – Wolf (which might have been a play on its home town of Wolverhampton and the nickname of its football team), Vixen (there also was a Fox truck), Otter and Seal.

Birds were used more widely. Crossley had an Eagle, Hawk and a Condor. It also had an Arrow, which I know was a weapon and not a bird, but had to rename it Alpha (a Greek letter later used by Atkinson) after Dennis (which also had an Arrow) objected.

Dennis took Condor as one of its names, too, first on a truck and later on a six-wheel export bus which it also called Dragon and in that guise may be the only bus named after a mythical reptile. Other Dennis birds were Falcon (first used in 1939), Teal (a fifties export

An *Aberdonian* for a Kilmarnock company poses against Stirling Castle. This 1950s Albion model was a cut-price Leyland Tiger Cub, 'saluting the legendary thrift of the citizens of Scotland's northern city'. It has an Alexander body, built in Stirling.

AEC decided to call its mid-1950s integral Park Royal-bodied single-decker the *Monocoach* 'but lilies were being gilded here as it really was a bus'. This is a 1954 Northern General example.

bus) and Pelican (an unsuccessful mid-1950s of prey in the 1960s with the Swift (recycled by Leyland in the 1980s) and Merlin, but Burlingham's Seagull coach was named after an operator in its home town of Blackpool.

After Burlingham's demise, Duple Northern turned from birds to insects with the Firefly and Dragonfly – apt choices as, in the natural world, these exotic and beautiful creatures live short lives in which they attract great attention.

Aggressive images

The subtlety of Leyland's double-deck giants was eclipsed by some overtly aggressive images of power from other manufacturers. Like Commer's Avenger (later used on a Hillman/Chrysler car), Commando and Invader; Guy's Warrior, Conquest, Victory and Invincible; Halley's Conqueror (which didn't); Plaxton's Crusader (later used by Willowbrook and, in the 1990s, by Wright's); Dennis's Dominant of 1951

(followed more successfully by Duple in 1972) and the Dominator in 1977.

There are wits who would have you believe the Dennis Dominator is the only bus named after a British prime minister – Margaret Thatcher having seemed to dominate the life of her husband Denis.

For sheer naked aggression and apparent lack of good taste, it's hard to match the name of Morris Commercial's Dictator. In mitigation, Morris might have moderated its nomenclature had the reputations of Messrs A Hitler, B Mussolini, J Stalin and F Franco been more clearly understood when the Dictator was launched in 1930.

Not that it was the only purveyor of images of global domination. Leyland's Worldmaster may be meant to convey export ambitions, but the wrong ears might interpret the message in a more sinister fashion. Worldmaster was but one example of several manufacturers' use of master-suffixed names: AEC had Routemaster and Bridgemaster, Duple its Roadmaster (more successful as a Dinky toy than a real coach), Rowe its Hillmaster, Plaxton its Viewmaster and Foden the Bandmaster after the company's renowned brass band.

Royalty, aristocracy and Empire have also been well represented, ranging from Thornycroft's Boadicea in the 1920s to the early 1950s revivalism of Duple's Britannia and Elizabethan and Park Royal's various attempts to sell coaches called Royalist. Morris Commercial had Imperial and Viceroy – the latter also used by Duple in the 1960s as a successor for its Viscount; Vulcan had Duke, Duchess, Countess, Prince, Princess and Emperor; Windover built the Kingsway coach; and Sunbeam commemorated two ethnic groups of the Indian subcontinent with its Pathan and Sikh.

The Guy Arab, always seeming incongruous with the

One of the last in a long line of distinguished Guy *Arabs*, Chester Corporation No 36, a 1965 Arab V with 73-seat Massey bodywork.

Gavin Booth

The *Fleetline* name was given to Daimler's 1960 rear-engined double-deck chassis, but later a single-deck Fleetline was offered. This East Kent (ex-Maidstone & District) example with Marshall two-door body, is seen in Dover in Sealink livery.

Gavin Booth

company's Red Indian radiator cap, may also have been inspired by one of the peoples of the erstwhile Empire, but there was no doubt about the inspiration behind Crossley's Dominion and Empire, the only trolleybuses honoured with names. Did anonymity accelerate the early demise of the silent trolley?

Military imagery

Other manufacturers' military imagery included the Harrington Cavalier, Grenadier and Legionnaire, the Duple Commander, Trooper and Yeoman and AJS Pilot, Commodore and Admiral or such weaponry as AEC's Sabre, Dennis's Arrow, Dart, Pike (unless, of course, it's a freshwater fish), Lance, Lancet, Mace and Javelin. And the general message of endurance and superiority is easy to recognise in Plaxton's Elite, Supreme and Paramount or Maudslay's Marathon.

Coach manufacturers often used a different sort of imagery to promote their products, one that appealed beyond their immediate customers to trippers, hirers

and holidaymakers who might judge a coach by the
name it carried. Often, this exotic image – certainly for
coach passengers in the 1950s or 1960s – was sheer
escapism.

Like the Latin romance of Duple's Vista and Vega
and their various Super, Bella and Major derivatives
on Bedford chassis, its Alpine Continental and
Caribbean, Yeates's Europa and Fiesta or Weymann's
Castilian, Fanfare, Amethyst and Topaz – the last two
hardly jewels in their manufacturer's crown if sales are
a fair measure of their success.

Plaxton's Panorama conveyed a similar image of
good views through its large windows, while models
like the Duple Laser and Willowbrook Spacecar
suggested something futuristic – a variation on MCW's
stellar theme of bus bodies called Orion, Aurora and
Hermes and Leyland's Comet of 1948 which recycled a
name first used on a wartime tank. Duple totally
reversed the effect by giving the Vega body the ancient
world name of Corinthian when it was fitted on a
Commer Avenger – and calling it a Yeoman on a Ford
Thames Trader and Roe's Dalesman was rooted firmly
in its native Yorkshire.

Humdrum

And romance gave way to humdrum when British
placenames were honoured by bus manufacturers.
Surprisingly few cities have been honoured by a bus
named after their citizens – just Crossley's prewar
Mancunian (the name was later adopted by
Manchester Corporation for its trend-setting 1968
double-deckers), Albion's lightweight Aberdonian

(saluting the legendary thrift of the citizens of
Scotland's northern city where joke books used to
show empty streets on charity flag days) and Guy's ill-
starred Wulfrunian which was hardly the best way of
honouring Wolverhampton or Wulfruna, the Mercian
king's sister who refounded its monastery in 994.

London only got a Londoner when London
Transport tried to make its first DMS-class Fleetlines
sound interesting, but one of its northern suburbs was
honoured when Duple, based there, called its Bedford
OB bus body the Hendonian – surely the most
parochial of all bus names. Plaxton took the name of a
river local to its Scarborough factory for a succession
of Derwent buses and Marshall honoured its home city
of Cambridge and its river with various Cam-prefixed
names like Cambrette and Camair.

In a similar vein, others used themed names without
a geographical connection, hence Daimler's only foray
into named buses spawned the Freeline, Fleetline and
Roadliner, but it confused too many potential buyers
into talking about Freeliners and Fleetliners.
Strachans' 1960s body range included a Pacesaver and
Paceline and MCW produced the Metropolitan (first
as a sixties coach, later as a double-decker), Metrobus,
Metroliner and Metrorider.

From all this, there seems to have been a constant
urge to suppress these products' true identity, as

One of Daimler's few named models, the *Roadliner*, the unhappy mid-1960s rear-engined chassis; this prototype has a Duple *Commander* body, one of many vehicles to carry military-type names.

Metrobus is the closest any of them comes to being called a bus or coach. The most notable exception to this habit was with lowheight double-deckers whose technical virtues were their biggest selling points.

Either that or the manufacturers just aped Bristol which, without the freedom to sell its trendsetter in the commercial market, was still proud enough of its achievement to christen the 1949 LDX as the Lodekka. Dennis built it under licence as the Loline (Gilford had sold a Low Line coach in the 1920s which was only low by the standards of its day), Leyland called its prototype rear-engined 'deckers Low Loaders, Albion's lowheight version of the Titan PD3 was the Lowlander (combining reference to its height with its lowland Scottish parentage) and AEC produced the Bridgemaster.

AEC also followed the functional route by calling its mid-1950s integral single-decker the Monocoach – but lilies were being gilded here as it really was a bus and AEC seemed scared to call it Monobus.

Did any of this make the slightest difference? Did operators really buy a bus or coach because they liked its name and did passengers notice or care whether they rode in a Regent, an Arab or a plain, unnamed K5G?

As I hinted, it may have helped a little in the coach market but for busmen it probably did little more than distinguish competing or complementary models. The sheer bluster of Guy's Invincible didn't save it from being beaten by Leyland's Titan or Daimler's unnamed CH6 and it's salutory to remember that most postwar front-engined Leyland Titans are better remembered as PD1s, PD2s and PD3s than they ever were by a model name that seldom appeared on its bonnet or radiator.

But there must be something in it. One American mass-produced import of the 1920s, R E Olds's Reo Speedwagon, inspired a pop group to take the name for itself (spelling out Reo as R E O) and motor industry hot gossip has it that Mercedes-Benz, which is adopting names to complement those confusing numbers as it updates its commercial vehicle range, is prepared to pay Volvo some hard earned Deutschmarks to release the Fleetline name it inherited from Leyland's acquisition of Daimler.

Perhaps that will sweep away a few prejudices as *Classic Bus* readers contemplate the buses of the 21st century. ■

THE ONES THAT
GOT AWAY

The first one to get away was EOG 260, the last ex-Birmingham Corporation Leyland TD6c in the fleet of McLennan of Spittalfield. In retrospect, it is a pity that 17-year-old Jasper Pettie was unable to contemplate the costs involved in buying a bus like this in 1962.

Jasper Pettie

JASPER PETTIE describes the buses that, despite every effort, slipped through his hands

IN 1970, at the age of 25, I took the plunge and bought my first bus. It was a logical, carefully considered step – for several years I had contemplated owning my own vehicle and had even dabbled briefly in bus preservation with a group in Canada. But now, I had decided, was the time to act, to come out of the closet and nail my colours to the mast for all the world to see.

This (for me) cataclysmic event had been preceded by one or two half-hearted attempts to save a suitable candidate for posterity. The one that particularly sticks in my mind was on a visit to McLennans of Spittalfield where I was caught in the act (by the chief engineer no less) inspecting the last ex-Birmingham Corporation Leyland TD6c in their ownership. McLennans had bought a sizeable fleet of these in the early 1950s and they had been a common sight in rural Perthshire during my childhood. EOG 260 had soldiered on as a

driver trainer for several years after its contemporaries had all been scrapped, and to a wet-behind-the-ears 17-year-old, didn't look in half-bad condition with its idiosyncratic Metro-Cammell straight staircase body, although I noticed that its torque converter had been replaced with more conventional cog-swapping apparatus. 'It's yours for £75, taxed and all,' said this voice at my elbow, as if echoing my thoughts. I suppose other 17-year-olds have bought buses and have overcome all the difficulties of cost, storage, restoration etc. against all the odds and survived to tell the tale, but, sad to say, I wasn't going to be one of them. I chickened out. I remember thinking at the time that someone else would be bound to snap up such a lovely specimen. But no-one did – which explains why there are no surviving examples of the TD variant supplied exclusively by Leyland to the specifications of the largest municipal bus fleet outside London, at least to my knowledge. (I'd be more than happy if somebody were to prove me wrong!)

I had decided, because I had had so many happy encounters with the marque during my formative years, that my intended purchase would have to be a

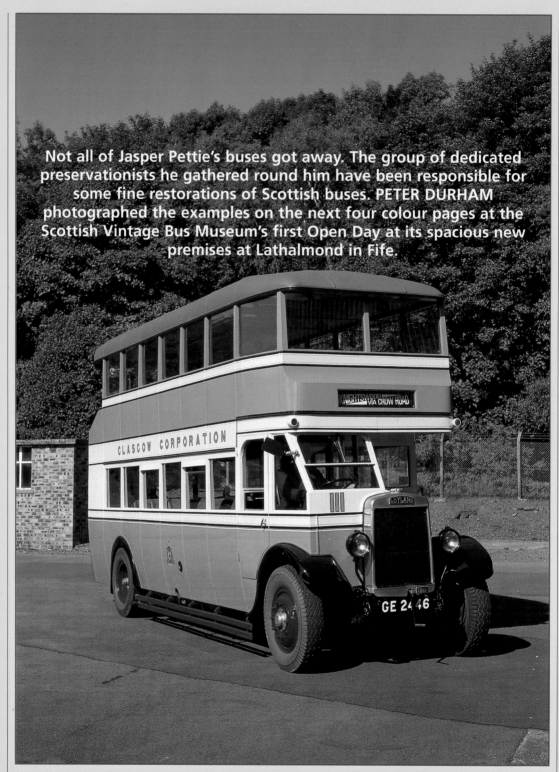

Not all of Jasper Pettie's buses got away. The group of dedicated preservationists he gathered round him have been responsible for some fine restorations of Scottish buses. PETER DURHAM photographed the examples on the next four colour pages at the Scottish Vintage Bus Museum's first Open Day at its spacious new premises at Lathalmond in Fife.

The current flagship of the SVBM collection is Glasgow Corporation No 111, a 1928 Leyland Titan TD1 with Leyland open-staircase 51-seat lowbridge body. No 111 was part of a batch of 100 for Glasgow in 1928/9, and when it was withdrawn in 1940 it was sold to the Civil Defence for use as an ambulance. In the mid-1980s it was discovered in use as a static caravan in Kent and brought north to Scotland where it was completely rebuilt with the assistance of the Scottish Bus Group and Strathclyde Buses.

VD 3433 was one of 110 Leyland Lion LT5A built for Central SMT and its associate fleet Lanarkshire Traction in 1934. It was sold by Central in 1945 and bought, along with another eight, by W Alexander & Sons. They received new 36-seat Alexander semi-utility style bus bodies in 1946 and were fitted with six-cylinder engines in place of the original four-cylinder units. VD 3433 became No P721 and operated on Perth City services and for Alexanders subsidiary David Lawson Ltd. After withdrawal in 1959 it was sold to a showman and was bought for preservation in 1973.

In the early part of World War 2 the Ministry of Supply froze the production of passenger vehicles, but in 1942 partially-built vehicles, and vehicles that could be assembled from parts in stock, were 'unfrozen', and DSG 169 is a result of this decision. Leyland assembled 196 of its current Titan TD7 double-deck chassis, and one of the previous TD5 model; DSG is the TD5. It carries an Alexander body built on Leyland frames and outwardly a prewar Leyland product, and was delivered to SMT, Edinburgh in 1942. It was converted to open-top layout in 1959 and was eventually sold in 1973, for preservation. It returned to Scotland in 1980 and in the course of a major body overhaul received a new roof from an ex-Ribble Leyland PD2. It was repainted in the blue livery worn by SMT buses until 1949.

Another bus that would be a valuable addition to the ranks of preserved buses would be a Leyland Tiger TS8 Special, a once-familiar type in many parts of Scotland. The short-length driver's cabs meant that the Alexander bodies had seats for 39 instead of the normal 35. This was the 1940 bus from the Alexander fleet (though in Lawson's maroon) that Jasper nearly bought in Perthshire.

A J Douglas

The ill-fated attempts to save this ex-Edinburgh Corporation 1935 Daimler COG6 with Metro-Cammell bodywork are described in the article. It is seen here just off the A702 road near Biggar in April 1968.

Jasper Pettie collection

Another Edinburgh bus that nearly found itself preserved was this 1938 Daimler COG5/Weymann, Edinburgh's prewar single-deck standard model, seen at Seacliffe in 1977.

Jasper Pettie

Guy Arab MkII or MkIII but as I was stalking suitable candidates an event took place which almost scuppered my plans. My father was friendly with a fruit farmer in deepest Perthshire who, in common with many in the area, ran buses in the harvesting season to transport the labour to the crop. He mentioned this to me, but not being up on matters bus-wise (my father, that is) was unable to describe the vehicles he'd seen on his last visit. I suggested to him that on his next trip he write down the registration numbers and, sure enough, a few weeks later, looking at his piece of paper, I could hardly believe what I saw. WG 9494 was a 1940 Leyland TS8 Special, that exclusively Scottish variant of the Tiger range. Several sizeable batches, all with very graceful Alexander semi-coach bodies, had been operated by Alexanders, SMT and Western SMT and were personal favourites of mine, and at one time were a familiar sight all over Scotland. Many were destined to survive for well over 20 years, but all presumed long gone. Here was a survivor right under my very nose!

I wasted no time in contacting the farmer, who indicated that despite the fact that he had sold it to a pair of itinerant scrappies for £50 two days before (it later transpired that my father had personally witnessed this transaction!) they had yet to collect it and there was a chance it could be saved. That very evening after work, I drove hell-for-leather to the farm only to find that the scrappies had taken the bus while the farmer was out, driven it to the nearest piece of waste ground and torched it half-an-hour before I got there. The Perthshire air was full of expletives!

History has a habit of repeating itself: some dozen or so years later a more exotic attempt to rescue another Scottish TS8 ended in rather similar circumstances, of which more later.

A sad loss

On the A702, a mile north of the town of Biggar, there stood a static caravan, unmistakably double-deck bus-shaped, which by the early 1970s had been a familiar landmark for many years. This had originated as Edinburgh Corporation No G12 (WS 6372), a 1935 Daimler COG6 with Metro-Cammell metal-framed body which was still basically complete apart from running units. Attempts to trace the owner of this vehicle proved surprisingly difficult until one of our number, fortuitously and quite by chance, met his son who confirmed that his father had long since given up holidaying in the beast and, yes, would do what he

The Cyprus Tiger, seen on the first visit, squeezed into a corner of the Larnaka yard, a fine example of a prewar SMT Leyland Tiger/Alexander rear entrance bus.

Jasper Pettie

This former Alexander all-Leyland Titan TD1 was found in the West Lothian hills in 1976, but itinerant scrap dealers beat the preservationists to it. At least Jasper Pettie now has a share in the splendid Glasgow Corporation TD1.

Jasper Pettie

London Transport built up a fleet of 435 utility Guy Arabs in the 1940s and when LT decided to sell them in the 1950s many operators bought them to augment their fleets. Edinburgh Corporation, just embarking on its tram-replacement programme, bought 60, removed the utility bodies, had the chassis refurbished, and fitted new 8ft wide Duple-Nudd 55-seat bodies with full-width fronts. The 60 buses gave good service in Edinburgh for some 15 years, and No 314 (JWS 594) experimentally received a Gardner 6LW engine in place of the normal 5LW unit. With its brothers it had also received Leyland-style glassfibre fronts. No 314 was retained for conversion to a tree-lopper, but this conversion never took place and it was bought in 1972 for preservation. It has been restored to its original frontal style, with 5LW engine. The chassis was formerly London Transport GLL 577.

Edinburgh Corporation had a long tradition of buying single-deckers with the traditional Scottish style of cutaway rear entrance. It needed a larger-than-normal single-deck fleet because of low railway bridges on important routes, and after the War continued to buy what were essentially newer versions of its prewar standard. Edinburgh had operated utility Guys during the War, and although it was anxious to buy its prewar Daimler/MCW combination, postwar vehicle shortages meant that it had to shop around. There were 15 unique Bristol L6B with Scottish-built Brockhouse bodies, 10 Daimler CVG6/Metro-Cammell, and 10 Guy Arab III with similar Metro-Cammell 35-seat bodies. The Guys were new in 1948 and ran until 1961; two buses were converted to driver training vehicles at this time and performed these duties until 1970. In 1970 both were bought for preservation, and one vehicle restored from the two.

Guy had some success in Scotland in the early postwar years. EVA 324 was new to Central SMT in 1950 with a Guy-built 33-seat rear entrance body, one of a batch of 12. Fitted with a Gardner 5LW engine, EVA 324 was withdrawn in 1962 and bought by a farmer in the Dundee area for transporting fruit-pickers. In 1978 it was purchased for preservation and is now restored in the Central red/off-white livery.

The classic Bedford OB helped many coach fleets to get back into business after the War. No SS 7501 was new in 1950 to Cleghorn of Haddington with the familiar Duple Vista body and was used on local service. The bus passed with the Cleghorn business to Ian Glass of Haddington and was sold in 1965 to a North Berwick farmer for transporting farm workers. It was bought for preservation in 1978 and completely restored over a period into the blue livery of another local OB operator, Wiles of Port Seton. It has since been used in the BBC television series 'Strathblair'.

could to secure the vehicle for us, but he did admit that relations between him and his father had become somewhat strained of late. Just how strained became woefully apparent very shortly thereafter, when a friend who lives in the area telephoned to say that the bus was no more – a local scrappie had been instructed to cut it up on site and no questions to be asked. Daimler COGs are very thin on the ground in preservation and as this type had formed the backbone of Edinburgh's prewar bus fleet we felt quite sore about this loss but much worse was to follow.

A few years later some of our number had run to ground a Bedford OB with an East Lothian history (eventually restored, this became the star of the TV series 'Strathblair', but that's another story) and this was being collected one fine summer evening from a farmyard near North Berwick. As usual, somebody had forgotten some vital piece of equipment or other and off we went in search of human habitation to scrounge whatever it was that we lacked. On rounding a corner we were confronted by a row of terraced farm cottages in front of which was another caravan, unmistakably Daimler, unmistakably Edinburgh, although this time unmistakably single-deck and inhabited – the owner and his wife were out enjoying the evening sunshine! We introduced ourselves – they had heard about our interest in the OB – and we were shown round. The bus had been in situ for some 20 or so years, we were informed, and on looking around I was struck by the retention of so many of the original bus fittings in the caravan conversion. The owner confessed to being a bit of an enthusiast as he had had a soft spot for the type when in service and with a flourish produced the front number plate – BWS 204 – which identified it as Edinburgh No A70, one of the 1938 batch of COG5s supplied to Edinburgh with Weymann B36R saloon bodies. He seemed most intrigued at the thought that someone would want to restore his bus to roadworthy condition once more, and revealed that as he and his wife were advancing in years the maintenance of his holiday home was becoming a problem and he would consider our offer. We parted firm friends with promises to keep in touch and I must confess that I thought he would honour his commitment. About a year later on revisiting the area, however, BWS 204 had vanished and literally no trace could be found. Our second bite at the cherry had also failed. To lose one Edinburgh Daimler was bad enough – to lose two was nothing short of carelessness bordering on the criminal. I still have fond memories of travelling on Edinburgh COGs as a child – as does your esteemed editor! – and needless to say no others have ever turned up since.

Win some, lose some

You might be forgiven for wondering, dear reader, why after such devastating disappointments I had not been locked up in some institution undergoing urgent treatment for severe depression or worse. During this time we were happily and successfully acquiring such gems, inter alia, an ex-Alexanders 1934 Lion LT5A (two), 1929 Tiger TS2 and an ex-Central SMT Guy Arab saloon, some of which have been subsequently restored and have become quite familiar on the rally circuit, but as every preservationist knows, you win some but boy, you have to be prepared to lose some.

I seemed to be doomed to failure when static caravans were involved for I was to encounter yet another similar event not long after. This time the bus was a Leyland TD1 and the location was the rather pretty village of Torphichen up in the hills above Bathgate in West Lothian. Said TD1 was located near a stream and in an almost inaccessible spot and it was learned that in 1949 it had been skidded into place on greased steel plates and used ever since as a summer chalet by an Edinburgh family, with whom contact was duly made. We were cordially invited to inspect the vehicle whose Leyland lowbridge body had deteriorated into a dangerous condition, but still possessed many valuable fittings useful as spares, although minus all running units. Ex-Alexander No R208 (FG 5335), the bus had come to that concern with the business of A & R Forrester of Lochgelly, one of a pair. It soon became apparent that the family now regarded the bus as a liability, and were delighted with the offer to dismantle it at no cost to themselves! Arrangements were made, a date was fixed and we duly arrived complete with tackle to be greeted with the sight of fresh air where the bus had been. Telltale marks on the ground confirmed our suspicions: once again, itinerant scrappies had beaten us to it and the family, under the impression that the scrappies were acting on our behalf, innocently gave them the go-ahead. Many years later, when we had discovered and were restoring Glasgow TD1 GE 2446, I had cause to reflect on more than one occasion how much simpler that exercise might have been had we had the opportunity to strip FG 5335 of useful body spares.

Cypriot Tiger

The near-miss that really stuck in my gullet, and still rankles when I recall it some 12 years on, started with a letter from Cyprus from a friend who was serving with the Army there. For many years, Cyprus had been a repository for tired-out British buses and commercials to eke out the twilight of their lives before being driven to a huge scrapyard on the outskirts of Larnaka at the south-east of the island. 'Scrapyard' is perhaps a misnomer as nothing ever seemed to be actually scrapped, and after 25 years it contained row upon row of mouth-watering gems such as Bedford OBs, Bristol J and L-type single-decks, ex-Birmingham Daimler COG5s minus their top decks, to name but a few, not to mention equally vast numbers of commercial vehicles both military and civilian. Moreover, the climate and lack of vandalism ensured

right people, and in no time I was staring at my quarry – CSF 228 – forlorn, derelict but intact, complete and eminently restorable. It just had to be repatriated.

Our main problem was in finding a shipping line which would take a bus as deck cargo and not charge an arm and a leg, not to mention run into tropical storms on the way home which might wreak damage to our pride and joy, or worse. Precedents for such a trip had already been set, but it was a question of finding the right ship at just the right time. The months slipped by and as we seemed to be making some progress it was decided to return to the island to make some on-the-spot arrangements. We were met by our Cypriot hosts who seemed more subdued than usual and we soon found out why. On arrival at the yard we found to our horror that since our last visit a fire started by a neighbouring farmer to burn chaff had got out

that deterioration did not set in nearly as quickly as it would have done in the UK.

My friend had managed to become acquainted with the yard owner and indeed had already been involved in the rescue and repatriation of several vehicles, but the object of his attention now was a prewar Leyland single-decker unidentifiable save for a fleet number (H217) on the inside front bulkhead; the fact it had a cutaway rear entrance led him to suspect that it might have a Scottish connection. Photographs of the bus subsequently confirmed my initial hunch: the bus was a 1939 Tiger TS8 with Alexander 34-seat body, absolutely original and still complete with seats, sliding roof, roof rack and rear steps as well as all the mechanicals. A visit just had to be arranged!

And so it was that we duly flew out of Heathrow on a dull November day, bound for sun, sea and scrapyards, full of anticipation. We were not to be disappointed. All three were in abundance as it turned out, my friend quickly made all the right noises to the

of hand and had swept through the yard. Now all the OBs, COG5s, Bristols etc were nothing more than charred ruins, most of these totally unrecognisable. We found our TS8, a twisted unsalvageable wreck amidst all this and there was nothing for it but to slink home on the first flight back, retire to lick our wounds, and consign the whole episode to history and experience.

Despite all these failures and near-misses I consider myself to be a fairly pragmatic soul – I will always counter these negative aspects by pointing out all the successful sorties I have been involved in that have resulted in vehicles going on to be restored to their former glory over the last 20-or-so years, but there is one thing that does niggle. Why is it that the ones that get away always seem to be the very last of their batches, and conversely, against all the odds, of a total of 25 1934/35 Leyland Lion LT5As rebodied by Alexander in 1945, for instance, I own two, and a third recently surfaced which we were invited to dismantle for spares? ■

THE PRIMROSE PATH

ROBERT E JOWITT
spent the formative years
of his youth falling in love
with – and on – the
Bournemouth trolleybuses; he
dwells here with fond if melancholy
nostalgia for vanished days of dalliance.

True love by the traffic lights. Jowitt hopes he bought her a bunch of flowers. Beyond is 1935 Sunbeam No 210

1950 BUT No 247 waits to depart for the wilds of Winton and Wallisdown. Sweetheart waits by the telephone boxes for Jowitt to make haste.

THE CURVING STREET, as I walk along it, looks much the same, with slightly crumbling Victorian villas discreet behind handsome trees and flourishing shrubberies, as it looked when one damp and grey March evening a quarter of century before I had entered a drive which led to one of those villas, a girl beside me.

The villa, formerly a family home of some pretension, had long since been broken up into flats. The girl and I had to enter her flat very circumspectly, for the landlord, once the victim of a wild party guest sliding down the bannisters to land feet first in his stomach, took a dim view of visitors. I suppose another reason for our caution was that I had fallen for this girl

because I could not possibly make up my mind between the one I had fallen for before her and the one before that.

Now as I enter that once-familiar drive to view the scene of that long gone folly I discover that the house has been torn down to make way for a roaring highway. This desecration of the scene of a fond if foolish passion sets me to reflect upon 'all the changing scenes of life' as the hymnologist puts it 'in trouble and in joy', and upon all the Victorian architecture which has been laid waste in Bournemouth since my youth there when I trod the primrose path of dalliance, and upon the slaughter of the primrose trolleybuses which had been such a part of my life and my romances.

I never lived in Bournemouth. I spent my childhood in Winchester, but I may say with some authority, from reference to my mother's diary, that I first saw the Bournemouth trolleybuses on 12 April 1947. I was just

This damp scene in May 1959, belying Bournemouth's record of sunshine, was almost certainly Jowitt's first photograph of a Bournemouth trolleybus and probably his only one depicting a 1935 Sunbeam with original fleet number and crest on the front. While several of her sisters were withdrawn at this stage No 105 survived to become 214. The bus stop, though generally informative, fails to say that 37 goes to Fisherman's Walk, merely implying it by innuendo.

All photos by Robert E Jowitt

Ex-Brighton Corporation 1947 BUT, fitted with typical Bournemouth destination layout, looks quite at home in its new surroundings, resting against a chock in Avenue Road.

The face of the 1958 Sunbeam MF2B. No 268 was easy to distinguish from all the rest by virtue of smaller characters on her number plate.

five. I have no doubt that as we drove through the streets of Boscombe my father, enthusiastic if not well-informed about trains and trams, pointed out the trolleybuses . . . and of course the old saloon tram which served as waiting room at Ilford Bridge. We stayed at a hotel called Manor Heath, originally built by the renowned and royally-patronised play-actress Lily Langtry as a residence for her mother, but, more pertinent from my mother's point of view, close to the home of a dear friend, a Scottish doctor's widow.

I expect we rode on the trolleybuses then, but this escapes mention in my mother's diary. Three years later my parents took a holiday flat at Milford-on-Sea, and from then on visits to Bournemouth became regular.

Encouraged by my father's enthusiasm I was deeply impressed by the fact that the trolleybuses carried no advertisements (outside) and bore no less than six municipal crests, upper and lower decks, front and rear. As I grew older and learned wisdom (some) and studied the pages of *Buses Illustrated* (which my father took for its tram coverage) I conceived that the trolleybuses with their full fronts and simple lines were

the height of modernity. The Sunbeams were then 15 years old, but they looked as new as the 1950 delivery of BUTs. I doubt that I noticed the difference at that stage; this was, say, 1951 when the BCT was expanding the virgin overhead along Castle Lane.

In 1956 the good Scottish widow produced a couple of Italian girls. I think we rode on a Hants & Dorset full-front open-top to Sandbanks but I remember better travelling with these dark-eyed charmers on a 1935 Sunbeam, on the front seats upstairs. The Scottish widow travelled on one of the lower-deck lateral seats over the double rear axle. I fell utterly and futilely for G, who naturally soon after returned to the sunny Genoese shore leaving my passion unrequited with all the anguish of first love. The seats of the Sunbeams were leather, or, as the original 1933 specification demanded, 'Connolly's best nad-buffed hide', while the lamps were bald bulbs in white holders. On the BUTs the seats were moquette, the lamp bulbs in 'butter dishes'.

In 1958 the family abandoned Winchester and the Milford flat for a house in New Milton, not a town for which I ever cared but convenient for my starting at the Bournemouth College of Art. By now I was seriously interested in public transport and on a trip to Germany had started taking photographs on my mother's prewar folding 620. From the studio where I worked on lettering and pattern design I could see the trolleybuses passing all the time – life and plant

Even when 25 years old and sagging with antiquity in the middle, the 1935 Sunbeams never looked out-of-date. In this 1960 view with recent alterations to the overhead layout in the Square No 213's apparent lack of destination is caused by the same light which catches the booms of the preceding trolleybus in her windscreen.

drawing classes were less strategically placed – and after classes I caught trolleybuses from the Lansdowne (where the Art College was then situated) to ride bit by bit over every route and draw a map of the overhead and photograph all the junctions.

From my mother's 620 I progressed in the next two years, via a folding 116 from a Holdenhurst Road junk shop – the negatives are very inconvenient for present day enlargers – to a 35mm Ilford Sportsman. I am pleased to boast, 35 years later, that even then I took end-on and broadside views of buses and filled my pictures with architecture and humanity as well as taking 3/4-front record shots . . .

Exploring the trolleybus routes was a bit like looking at the rings of a tree trunk, starting with the high Victorian centre and working out through Edwardian and between-the-wars architecture to modern bungalows. Part of the Castle Lane route went through open fields.

Respectability and opulence

Apart from this rural ride the routes ran entirely through shopping streets or residential zones of varying degrees of respectability and opulence largely sprinkled with hotels and B&Bs. The Bournemouth system had none of the slums and dark satanic mills of the systems up north, it was entirely prim (as well as primrose). Another feature of note, considering Bournemouth's raison d'être as seaside resort, was that only at one point did the trolleybuses come within sight of the sea, at Bournemouth Pier, on summer only services . . .

Fate was kind in depositing me in Bournemouth in this era. True, the older Sunbeams were being withdrawn and dumped near Weymouth for breaking, but the hardier specimens flourished though renumbered and with fewer and smaller municipal crests; worse still, perhaps, three Sunbeams were converted to open-toppers. Deprived of front stairs and exit in favour of extra seats they probably earned good revenue from the trippers but at awful price in loss of beauty. For compensation, starting in 1958, came the delivery of the magnificent Sunbeam MF2Bs. These retained the traditional BCT rear-entrance/front-exit double-staircase layout but the exit was now 'front' instead of 'forward'; passengers with Pants & Corset bad habits continued to descend the back stairs and annoy the conductor while passengers becoming used to front-entrance buses were thoroughly confused. By some administrative quirk the new Sunbeams appeared with crest on the front at the same time as the old Sunbeams lost them.

The 30 new Sunbeams were joined by seven BUTs in 1959. I remember the shock of encountering what looked first of all almost exactly like a BCT BUT but on only two axles and with no forward exit. They proved to be 1947-8 vehicles secondhand from Brighton Corporation and Brighton Hove & District, and though smaller than their Bournemouth sisters they carried as many passengers, with 56 seats. The Bournemouth habit of front stairs cost a lot in seating. Fitted with BCT destination displays the ex-Brightonians looked thoroughly at home, but I suppose they well might; a newspaper report at the time cited Brighton and Bournemouth along with Blackpool as the three most immoral towns in England.

Myself all virtuous, I allowed my fancy to stray a little from the path of true love for trolleybuses. If I came in by train and walked from the Central station along Holdenhurst Road I passed the Shamrock & Rambler depot where all the orange/cream butterfly grille Duple Vegas were graced with names, which I assiduously wrote down. Ajax, Apollo, Atlas, Jason, Orpheus, Pegasus, Perseus, Titan; Alpha, Beta, Gamma, Delta, Epsilon, Iota, Kappa, Lamda, Omega, Sigma, Theta, Zeta; Capricorn, Leo, Taurus, Uranus, Virgo; Panther, Puma and Wasp! Sometimes my father drove me in our 1953 Ford Prefect to Somerford where I caught a route 1 MCW Leyland of 1950, full-fronted and dual-staircased. I preferred the prewar version with its proper radiator; a ride on one of these was a

1935 Sunbeam No 207 (formerly No 62), here with the Avenue Road (or the Square) terminus frogs between the 28/29/35 and 30/31 overhead loops plainly shadowed on her flank, was unique, at least after the 1959 withdrawals if not before, for the absence of a 'via' blind alongside the route number screen.

special treat. The Burlingham-bodied full-front 1949 Leyland single-deckers were equally desirable but I never recall catching one.

I sometimes caught Hants & Dorset buses, and hasten to mention this before my better-informed reads wonder why I haven't. However, I paid them scant attention, for they were the same Bristols I could see anywhere else, boring compared with the exotic elegance of the older BCT designs; I have to add I heeded equally little any post-1950 BCT buses for similar reasons. Nevertheless if I went into Bournemouth by train my day-return ticket entitled me to travel back by Hants & Dorset bus. The ticket stated the fact plainly, but more than once it came as a shock to such conductors as felt like arguing the point.

Some confusion

Of two main routes serving New Milton from Bournemouth the 20 had the great advantage of actually passing our gate, while even the 19 was nearer than the railway station. To the unwary or less-informed traveller (not like the readers of *Classic Bus*) H&D's route 20 was a source of some confusion as like BCT's trolleybus 20 it ran along Christchurch Road.

An elderly acquaintance of my mother's, known confusingly enough first of all as Gladys Lear and subsequently as Molly Ormerod, was attempting to reach New Milton and accordingly waved down a 20 and demanded of the condutor if he was bound thither. Alas, it was a trolleybus! 'We haven't got the wires out there yet!' the conductor cried. Gladys, or Molly, neither appreciating nor understanding his flippancy, was left frustrated on the pavement . . .

While such mishap naturally never befell me I was always frustrated at this period by my inability, through virtue or timidity, to catch an art student. Those girls with their multi-petticoated skirts and stiletto heels were far too sophisticated, and considered me odd because I wore a Leeds Tramways cap-badge on my lapel . . . not that they minded its position, it was the reason for wearing it all all which puzzled them.

In my second year I bought a pair of tight jeans and occasionally took a shy first-year girl on a trolleybus to

The last-ever 25 turns from Ashley Road into Christchurch Road on the suitably wet night of 12 September 1965. 1950 BUT No 242 has the unattractive new sans-serif fleet numbers.

When this picture was taken in 1960 it was very rare to see nothing but 1958 Sunbeam MF2Bs, though in later years there was no option! The antiquity of this view is proven by the tramway-style fleet numbers. The scene is at the Square, with a 25 heading up Commercial Road on the left, and Avenue Road in the centre.

Sunbeams from above. This view from Royal London House at the Lansdowne in 1964 shows passengers very properly entering at the rear and alighting at the front in true Bournemouth fashion

With heart divided between two, Jowitt photographed one on one side of Christchurch Road and the other on the other. The resulting montage did not please either of them. Also included are No 296 of 1962 and No 264 of 1958.

Boscombe for lunch in a cheap chip shop, but we never progressed beyond pea fritters and Ashley Road.

Nor did my studies conspicuously progress. I was passable at pattern and lettering but far from brilliant at life or plant. I had a few months off and my affections returned to girls I had known at 'League of Pity' dances in Winchester . . . with intervals for German trams and French buses.

I still kept up however with my college friend Ron and one evening when he and I were eating chips at the Lansdowne we saw a trolleybus dispole – the Lansdowne was a great place for this – and then gradually slip backwards downgrade with booms waving aloft and above a span wire before the driver

pulled up. The bamboo retriever was useless in such case; more and more trolleybuses queued up behind. As an ex-art student I drew a quick sketch of the scene on Ron's pad – I must have it somewhere still – for I had no camera with me and anyway it was dark.

I wrote a graphic account of this, far longer than this succinct summary, to my current Winchester girlfriend at her Convent School. I know for a fact that the Reverend Mother thought fit to read all my letters to this girl and I am pleased to think she had to wade her way through the several pages of brilliant essay on dispolement.

At Christchurch the trams had simply reversed in the street, but this didn't do for the trolleybuses so a turntable was provided in an inn yard, almost unique in trolleybus annals. Here the conductor seems to be making his life difficult by turning the trolleybus with one hand while holding down one boom with the other. The photo, in the last year of trolleybus life, shows 1959 Sunbeam No 287 clad with advertisements; while the sentiment of the main one is admirable the effect of both on the appearance of the vehicle is utterly deplorable.

The best-looking motor buses in Bournemouth were surely the 1939-MCW bodied Leyland TD5s. Seen here in 1960, not long before withdrawal, No 18 looks pretty smart at 21 years old. In the background is the tower of Plummers department store on the point between Old Christchurch Road and Gervis Place.

A little later, at about the time my romance with the Convent girl was drawing to a close (for other reasons besides my devotion to trolleybuses), my good Ron prevailed upon me to do two things; firstly to accompany him to the South Western Hotel where in a room above the stables art students held jazz hops; and secondly, in view of my increasing interest in photography, to consider returning to art college for a photographic course. At the jazz hops I became involved with sweet brown-haired grey-eyed C from Springbourne. The die was cast, C was everything. I started on the photography course.

My parents bought me a *de rigueur* Rolleicord, destined to be my faithful servant for a score of years thereafter.

C was not in fact an art student, she had a respectable job, but she followed closely the ways of the Bohemians, perhaps in rebellion against a tyrannical father. Like the girl before she had been Convent-educated; it was ever my lot, with an anti-Papist father, to fall in love with RC girls. C and I spent many hours in the front seat of the Ford Prefect outside her house arguing about the Pope and the Bible and Catholic doctrine. Bulleid Pacifics hurtled passed just behind the iron railings; beyond, on the depot-only route to Southcote Road, the trolleybuses sometimes punctuated our discussion by dispoling on the sharp corner.

Meanwhile, as the prewar Leylands were converted to ugly open-tops and the slightly younger and form-erly pristine Guy Arabs were cut down to single-deck open-tops or works vehicles the BCT took delivery of its final nine MF2Bs. Buses Illustrated states categoric-ally that the first, No 296, arrived on 16 July 1962. I saw one of them being towed in along Christchurch bypass. It may have been No 296 but I think more probably it was No 301, the last, I believe, to be delivered, though No 303 had the highest number . . .

In my first days at art college some of the old fleet-numbers must still have been about, but I learned to love the new numbers. Brought up on Hymns Ancient & Modern, and having read Gordon Stowell's History of Button Hill, I knew No 277 as 'Nearer my God to Thee', No 266 as 'Lead Kindly Light' and No 231, 1936 Sunbeam, my favourite, was 'Forever with the Lord.'

By now I knew the idiocyncracies of certain old Sunbeams as well as I knew the vagaries of C No 207 had no rear 'via' destination box, and so on.

I took C in the Ford Prefect to look at trams in Germany. Her father had fought the Hun at Arras or somewhere. He didn't like me.

Guy Arabs, though lacking the individuality of other Bournemouth buses, looked very smart in BCT livery. No 34, with 1943 Park Royal body, is speeding along Christchurch Road in 1960 on a rather vague-looking working.

I regret to have to say that despite the delights of trams in Germany and, a year later, in Austria, and despite how well we agreed on most issues even to the extent of joining a 'Homes before Roads' campaign and marching below the trolleybus wires with banners protesting agains the ravishing of Bournemouth by road schemes, C and I continued to argue about Catholicism and her father continued to dislike me. As I started my third year my eye was caught by first-year P, a golden-haired Pre-Raphaelite beauty who lived close to Pokesdown trolleybus depot.

Torn by indecision

Thereafter I was torn by indecision, sometimes with C, sometimes with P, ever with trolleybuses hissing past in the background, and the primrose path grew painful thorns of doubt and sorrow. Months later, as I said at the beginning, I sought a way out with S, another third-year, who had the distiction of having been run over in her childhood by a London bus. I hoped for the disfigurement that it had wrought on her leg, that it was a worthwhile bus such as an LT . . .

Nor S nor C nor P are by me now. 'Might-have-beens' provide fascinating and even entrancing speculation, but I cannot grumble at my present lot.

When I had finished my photography course I decided I did not want to photograph bourgeois weddings and I set out to earn my living as transport author and photographer, with additional and necessary income from part-time jobs. I even applied to become a conductor on the trolleybuses, but the BCT considered me too bright to be likely to stick to it!

Ironically enough in recent years my part-time jobs have mainly been driving psvs for rural Herefordshire firms, not least an operator rejoicing in the title of Primrose Motors, but indeed I might not have stuck to BCT conducting for the trolleybus system started to shrink. P and I rode on the last 25 on a night of suitably heavy rain; Holdenhurst Road deprived of trolleybuses was dreadful, and I couldn't take trolleybus to Westbourne any more to visit the wonderful secondhand bookshops in the Arcade.

The Winton and Moordown routes went next, I think. I had come to know them intimately while driving an almost brake-less Morris Commercial delivering greengroceries to the incredibly squalid kitchens of some of Bournemouth's smartest hotels. Even as the system withered (like the hotel vegetables?) a new traffic scheme in Southbourne required a lot of alterations to the overhead and the use of a seldom-employed turning circle as a one-way main route, but this entertaining extravagance lasted only three months, whereafter arrangements reverted to the former pattern . . . for little more than another year, however. Soon the moment had to come when the Southbourne and Ilford routes had to go, and the picturesque trolleybus turntable in the pub yard at Christchurch be put out of commission.

By now operations were reduced entirely to MF2Bs, some shamefully despoiled by upper-deck advertisements.

I wasn't there for the final demise of the trolleybuses at Easter 1969. I said goodbye to them quietly and sadly a little bit earlier while they were still running, as

In 1950 the motor bus fleet was almost doubled by 30 MCW-bodied Leyland Titan PD2/3s. With full fronts, dual stairs and rear-entrance front-exit layout they were close sisters of contemporary trolleybuses and thoroughly Bournemouthian. The dirty heap in front of No 119 in Holdenhurst Road is a last trace of the 1963 blizzard.

19 June 1969, Stour Road, Christchurch. Ex-Huddersfield AEC motorbus converted to BCT tower wagon and long a faithful and familiar supporter of the upkeep of BCT overhead, now has to reverse its role and pull the wires down . . . for ever.

if they might run for ever. At the death I was out in Spain with P, looking at London Q1s risen from the dead with various unlikely backgrounds of iron-ore mountains and florid cathedrals and monstrous giant aloes.

I had to hope that the Bournemouth Sunbeams, 10 or less years old, would share this happy fate, but there must have been a lack of pesetas or a change in Spanish transport politics. As I had seen the Sunbeams towed in new and lovely a few years before, now I saw them towed away behind old cut-down buses to be dumped in a Yorkshire scrapyard. Thus do the dreams and hopes and loves of youth die!

In the next few years, after three seasons driving on the 'Noddy Train' at Hengistbury Head, my connections with Bournemouth were severed. Not counting preserved specimens, the last vehicle I saw from the days of my youth was 'Apollo', no longer named but still in orange and cream livery, at a New Age Travellers' festival in May 1994, not long before it was impounded by the police – and presumably broken up. As for Bournemouth itself, on the rare occasions of my returns, the buses seemed much more yellow than the primrose of days of yore, pubs where we had drunk pints straight down – including the South Western – were demolished, and a great swathe had been cut through the residential streets. 'Homes before Roads' had failed. The house where S once lived had yielded as surely as the trolleybuses to the god and the scourge of the 20th century; the bypass had obliterated the primrose path. ∎

19 September 1969, out in the middle of the New Forest. Two
cut-down Leyland buses tows away one of the Sunbeam MF2Bs,
en route for a Yorkshire scrapyard.

No RM254 in Surbiton on the 65 route in July 1978 before receiving its 'Showbus' treatment.

Geoff Rixon

COVER STORY

GEOFF RIXON recalls the life of front cover star, RM254

RM254, built in March 1960, was delivered to West Ham garage in April 1960 to start its service life replacing trolleybuses. This was the first Routemaster fitted with 'quarter-light' opening front windows and like all other London Transport vehicles it worked from various garages around the capital, including Clapton and Croydon. In September 1977 it was transferred to Norbiton (NB) garage for use on the 65 route between Ealing and Chessington. Living in the Hampton Court area all of my life, I used to visit a section of this route at Surbiton, taking colour slides of the buses, 254 included. Who would have thought that a few years later I would be one of her owners.

In the early 1980s quite a few LT garages were paying special attention to 'pet' vehicles, mainly Routemasters, in order that they could attend rallies around the country. In most cases these vehicles were restored to 1960s condition, with gold fleetnames, cream bands and front brake cooling grilles. Norbiton selected RM254 as its 'Showbus'.

The bus stayed at Norbiton until August 1982 when it was due for a full overhaul at Aldenham works. Norbiton at this time was due to lose its RM allocation during a major garage rebuild, with vehicles moving to nearby Kingston. Passing Kingston garage one day I saw RM254 receiving some attention and began chatting to the staff working on the vehicle, who were getting her ready for the North Weald rally in May 1983. This was my first direct involvement with the vehicle. As a self-employed cabinetmaker, I offered to make a display board to carry the plaques which are given to visitng vehicles at rallies up and down the country. In return I was invited to join them at North Weald.

By the end of the year there were rumours of plans to withdraw the RMs from the area within 12 months. Rather than see RM254 go for scrap a group of us began to think of trying to purchase the bus from LT when they no longer wanted it.

January 1984 saw the imminent closure of Kingston garage. Norbiton, having been rebuilt at around £4million, was ready for the vehicles to return, 254 included. News also reached us that the vehicle could come up for sale in August that year.

We thought that purchase of the vehicle was going to be an easy process. We were sadly mistaken, as at the time London Buses would not sell any vehicles to groups or individuals, fearing that a competitor might be in the wings. Luckily Norbiton Sports and Social Club agreed to purchase the vehicle on our behalf upon withdrawal. However a member of staff with Bus Sales at Chiswick told us that although we could purchase a Routemaster bus we could not choose which one! A disappointment, but we carried on regardless.

One evening Paul Morris, a mechanic on the Norbiton staff, came to me with some bad news. LT wanted the vehicle to stay in service for another 12 months. So the rumours of RMs leaving the area were deferred as well! Fund-raising continued.

Sometime in early 1985, the running shift foreman at Norbiton handed me a letter from one Michael Dryhurst who had spotted the vehicle in service in pristine condition and was wondering if any plans were afoot to save the vehicle. Subsequently he joined the group who were planning just that.

On a lunchtime visit to Norbiton in June 1985 I was told that the man in charge of Bus Sales was about. I approached him and asked when it might be possible for us to have the vehicle. Following a two-minute phone call to the licensing department he gave us the good news that we could purchase RM254 on Friday 3 August that year, when the 71 route was going opo. This came as an amazing relief. There were just four of us left in the group at this stage and funds had reached about £3,000. This comfortably covered the asking price of £2,150.

RM254 ended 25 years of service life on 3 August when it entered Norbiton garage with running number NB171, on route 71 at 18.25 and the blinds were removed(!). The following Sunday it was taken by a member of the running shift to Turnham Green where the radio and other special fitments were removed. Then the following Wednesday it was taken to Bus Sales at the old AEC works in Southall where it was

Just out of Aldenham in September 1982, No RM254 in 'Showbus' condition in heavy traffic in Kingston on the 71 route.

'officially' purchased and then driven back to Norbiton garage. With permission from the engineering manager we were allowed to keep the vehicle in the back of the now empty Kingston garage.

Now we were in the preservation business work began on replacing body panels, the worst being those which carried advertisements on the sides of the vehicle. These were purchased from Aldenham works and on our way to Aldenham via Old Oak Lane, and heading for the Edgware Road, my son and I were the only passengers, sitting in the lower saloon. My son was about to go upstairs when there was an almighty bang and a tearing noise! We stepped off the bus to find the roof piled up on the back seat. Disaster! The driver, regularly on Routemasters from Norbiton and Kingston, jumped out of the cab in a state of shock and said 'Sorry, I didn't see the low bridge sign!' We had hit the railway bridge which carries the Great Western line over Old Oak Lane at Acton. The same bridge has claimed the roofs of about 30 other LT vehicles in the past. Ever since this, the driver's colleagues have nicknamed him 'Topper'.

There was great feeling of panic; 'What do we do now?' We couldn't take it back to Kingston as the roof was piled too high to get it back in the garage. There was no alternative but to go on to Aldenham, the best place to be in these circumstances, where we now needed more than just eight new body panels!

The first assessment, from an expert, suggested that things weren't as bad as they looked. A repair could be effected fairly easily as none of the window uprights was damaged and only one pane of glass broken. It was a clean 'tin-opener' job just above the frames. As luck would have it, LT had just removed the roof from RM581 as it was being sold to a newspaper company for use as an open-topper.

Fund-raising had to start again in earnest as the cost was going to be high. Finally the bus received new front and rear domes and the whole operation took around two weeks to complete at a cost of £2,691. It

was driven, very carefully, back to Kingston, via a different route and with a different driver!

Preservation now began in earnest! Every evening and most weekends were spent in the back of Kingston garage, cold, damp and often in the dark, where every panel and strip was removed to be cleaned of several layers of paint, back to bare metal. Then in January 1986, in temperatures of -12c, RM 254 was driven to LPC Coachworks, at Hounslow Heath for a quote to repaint it. With bodywork completed in April it returned to Hounslow for painting at a cost of £1,800.

While at LPC it became clear that it couldn't return to Kingston, and it subsequently lived in various temporary homes – at Clapham garage, at a film storage warehouse near Southall (courtesy of Michael Dryhurst), then back to Norwood. During this time we restored all the interior of the bus, replacing the flooring and the seating.

Michael Dryhurst had been in bus preservation for some time and was keen to bring RT1 back from California to save it being turned into a burger bar! In order to do this, in 1986, he sold half his share of RM254. Incidentally, in 1989 we received two serious offers to buy RM254. Both in the region of £30,000. No sale!

In 1990 LT raised the price for vehicles being stored in Norwood so 254 spent 18 months at Fulwell. Then when LT closed the expensively-rebuilt Nortbiton we moved into the old Twickenham (AB) garage after contact with the Routemaster Owners & Operators Association. The Routemaster Heritage Trust (RHT), formed in April 1992, leased AB from the LT Properties Board, and hoped it might provide a permanent home for a growing collection of vehicles belonging to a number of preservation groups and individuals.

LT sold Twickenham garage to developers in 1994, but the RHT was offered seven months in Norbiton, by now empty and sold to the same developers. So RM254 was to return to where it was allocated 17 years previously. In January 1995 the RHT collection was dispersed and we moved into a new home under cover on a site near the old Hanwell London Transport garage. It is hoped that this 'home' lasts a little longer than some of the others!

The most recent work has been the addition of period advertisements, hand-painted on the sides of the vehicle. The designs were found by looking at many 1960s photographs and selecting those which caught our eye. The painting was carried out by a master signwriter.

Work continues to complete and maintain restoration to 1960s condition. It is rallied extensively and is admired by many, gaining a number of awards. Mechanically, RM254 has behaved impeccably. Paul Morris who has cared for the vehicle mechanics since its LT 'Showbus' days, is a perfectionist and it is a tribute to him that we have enjoyed so many miles of trouble-free rallying.

Having now reached retirement age, I'm able to see the results of many hears of excitement and disappointments. RM 254 in its present condition is a tribute to the design team from LT, but there's a lot of 'elbow grease' needed to keep it like it is! ∎

L IS FOR LEYLAND. Well, what else, especially as 1996 marks the centenary of the founding of the Lancashire Steam Motor Company. From small beginnings, this enterprise was to make the name of an obscure Lancashire town famous around the world as Leyland Motors, the successor to the short-lived Lancashire Steam Motor Co, exported buses and trucks to virtually every corner of the globe. (Globes, incidentally, don't have corners – but why let pedantry stand in the way of a well-established phrase.)

Leyland grew ever more successful. Its growth was gradual, but its decline relatively rapid. When Leyland Bus celebrated its 90th anniversary in 1986, who would have thought that 10 years later the only link with the Leyland name would be the Olympian – a double-deck chassis built in Scotland by a Swedish company?

M IS FOR MAUDSLAY, which had the distinction of being one of the most progressive and one of the most conservative British bus builders at different times. The Warwickshire firm dates back to 1905, and in 1935 introduced its highly innovative SF40, with set-back front axle and a seating capacity up to 40. It was available with petrol or diesel engines, the latter from Gardner. However by 1946 it was about the last manufacturer building petrol-engined heavyweights, with its highly conservative Marathon II. The superseding Marathon III was diesel-powered, but using an AEC driveline, and AEC acquired the company in 1948. That might have been the end; the last Maudslay buses were built in 1950, though that year it also built nine Regent IIIs for Coventry. Yet it went on to build specialist AEC models and axles, and indeed still exists at its Alcester site as a factory for Rockwell.

Two alphabet letters in one picture –
a *Maudslay* Marathon III with *Plaxton* bodywork.

N IS FOR NUMBERS. Buses have them. Lots of them. A chassis number certainly; a body number probably; a registration number; a fleet number. Organisations like the PSV Circle thrive on gathering these together into news-sheets and fleet histories. Computer-friendly systems mean that many fleet numbering schemes are just that. Numbers. Gone from many fleets are the complex lettering systems that sometimes were backed-up with logic, often not. One fleet that has dropped prefix (and suffix) letters is SMT; a few years ago its fleet included XCMM146A – that's a fleet number rather than a registration number. X meant toilet-fitted coach, C meant Citylink livery, MM meant a double-deck MCW, 146 was its number, and A was its depot, New Street Edinburgh. Today it would just be 146. (See also under Z)

O IS FOR ORION, the nearest equivalent of the Leyland National in the 1950s. Metro-Cammell Weymann's standard double-deck body, launched in 1952, was one of the first products to recognise the realities of the bus industry's decline from the postwar travel boom. It was light, it used mass-produced rather than hand crafted components and interior finishes and it was largely to its manufacturers' design rather than being a bespoke creation of proud municipalities or big companies. It also hit the market as people like Brush and Leyland pulled out of bus bodybuilding and went down a storm with municipals and BET fleets from Aberdeen to Plymouth, Swansea to Newcastle. Kit-built Orions went to Ulster and the design was adapted for Atlanteans and Fleetlines when the industry took to rear engines. In its original form, it came on Leyland, AEC, Guy, Daimler, Dennis and rebodied Bristol chassis, in highbridge and lowbridge form, with rear or forward entrances (both together in Bournemouth), full fronts or halfcabs, four bays or five and could be 27ft or 30ft long. You either liked or loathed its functional finish. Most memorably, an Edinburgh councillor wrote it off as a 'monstrous mass of shivering tin' and in the pages of Classic Bus, one Michael Dryhurst described it as a 'shapeless mastadon of featureless anonymity', but we know it also has its fans. Orion is also the brand name of Ontario Bus Industries whose curious lowfloor midibuses are found in North America (along-side its big single-deckers) and in Scandinavia. They're neither featureless nor anony-mous, but you either like or loathe their appearance, too.

The MCW Orion, widely disliked but looking presentable in Halifax green/orange/cream livery. A 72-seat 1959 Leyland PD3/4.

P IS FOR PLAXTON. Plaxton are the people who brought the British coach industry one of its great classics: the Panorama. The Panorama was a breath of fresh air when it first appeared in 1958. It abandoned all the fussy mouldings and convoluted curves of the earlier part of the decade – and introduced big windows, giving coach passengers an uncluttered view of the world around them.

When it was launched British coaches were limited to a maximum length of 30ft (shorter than most Dennis Darts!) and many still had centre entrances – an option on the Panorama. But what really puts the Panorama into context is a look at what preceded it. Five years earlier, for example, Bellhouse Hartwell was producing outrageous curved confections. Ten years earlier a halfcab coach was considered the last word in luxury.

And the Plaxton story has a happy ending. The Panorama has long since been consigned to history, but its builder continues to go from strength to strength.

Not Queen Line as such, in fact nothing really to do with it, but an ex-London Transport RT decked out in 'Victouriana' livery. Oh dear.

Q IS FOR QUEEN LINE. It was once said that when Green Line was set up, it registered all sorts of similar names to prevent others using them, but forgot one or two such as 'Queen Line'. Whether it did or not, the Queen Line element is irrelevant, because Queen Line Coastal Coaches had begun operating services from Willesden to the coast in 1928, two years before Green Line was registered. It merged in 1930 with Baldock Motor Transport, to form the snappily-titled Queen Line Coaches & Baldock Motor Transport, which ran under the Queen Line name primarily between London and Baldock, on a Green Line-style service. Almost inevitably, Queen Line's London service passed to Green Line (a year's free *Classic Bus* subscription for the best limerick!) in 1933, and the name shortened to Queen Line Coaches Ltd in 1934, by which time it ran '1 AEC Regal 32-seater sun saloon; 4 De Dion Bouton 28-seater saloons; 2 Tilling-Stevens sun saloons; 4 De Dion Bouton 25-seater saloons', and had a head office in 74 Park Hill, London SW4 (tel: Macauley 3381). It finally fizzled out in 1940. So it would appear that the story that the Queen Line name was used because it was one that Green Line forgot to register was just a load of old Baldock.

R IS FOR RUTLAND. No, not the county. The coach. Not a lot of them were built – probably three. The Rutland was built ('assembled' is probably a better word) by a company called Motor Traction Ltd of New Addington, Surrey. The first chassis, in 1953, had a front-mounted engine, but two Clippers, bodied by Whitson in 1954/5, had rear-mounted Perkins P6 engines and were therefore ahead of their time. So much so that no more were built.

Great Yarmouth to Plymouth 1951

ROY MARSHALL describes one of his early postwar marathons

Cyclists on a leisurely ride delay the crossing of the swing bridge by a Lowestoft Corporation AEC Regent bodied locally by Eastern Coach Works. Nine of these went to the Corporation, a tenth going to Ebor at Mansfield. Before the building of new housing estates the Corporation was restricted to the old tram route running along the coast from the north to the south of the town.

All photos by Roy Marshall

THE YEAR 1948 marked a significant change in my interest in buses for I was fortunate enough to have saved sufficient cash to replace a Box Brownie camera by a folding Zeiss Ikon Nettar which permitted variable speeds and apertures, although in those days of slow speed films 1/60th at f5.6 was common. Film became easily available; at first ex-RAF and later Italian. In 1949 I planned to cover the municipal systems out of reach of a day trip from Nottingham or based at relatives living near Halifax. This coverage had to be undertaken on my annual seven day leave; this apart from Good Friday and Bank Holiday Mondays being the extent of my entitlement until I moved into the municipal sector later in 1951. This year then was the chance to cover some of these systems and so on Saturday 16 June I travelled on the Trent express service from Nottingham to Great Yarmouth arriving in the early afternoon.

During the next seven days I travelled by bus, coach and train using accommodation in Great Yarmouth, Ipswich, Southampton and Exeter to visit additionally Lowestoft, Colchester, Portsmouth, Bournemouth and Plymouth. Great Yarmouth was busy with early holidaymakers and public transport was well patronised. At that time the fish docks were also busy, the smell in certain quarters being evidence of this. The blue and cream buses of the Corporation were quite impressive but as an AEC enthusiast I was disappointed to see that this make had not been favoured for many years, allegiance having passed to Leyland. Eastern Counties had nothing of interest to me which I had not previously seen in Peterborough.

A quiet Great Yarmouth promenade as No 12, a Corporation Massey-bodied Leyland Titan TD5 of 1939, heads for the Pleasure Beach. A similar vehicle, rebodied with a Northern Coachbuilders utility body, proceeds towards town. In those days Belisha beacon crossings were the norm – pre-dating the Zebras.

In 1942 Bristol built a number of complete vehicles to utility specification, unusual, being of six-bay construction. The conductor gives the impression that he had rarely if ever seen anyone photographing a bus before as No 35 loads outside W H Smith, a company then involved in circulating libraries.

The small Lowestoft Corporation fleet comprised only wartime Massey-bodied Guys and postwar Regents which I sampled on a ride to Pakefield so my visit there was only brief. At Ipwich the hotel porter explained that the room I was to occupy for one night was much sought-after in winter as one wall carried the chimney from the kitchen! This was not winter but I was too inexperienced to protest. Looking back I am amazed how I was able to cover the Corporation fleet quite well on arrival and then do the same in Colchester before returning to Ipswich for the night. Unfortunately the last prewar Ipswich trolleybus, of

more streamlined appearance to the others, was being worked on in the depot but a visit a few years later found it on service.

A further interest of mine at this time was trolleybus overhead equipment, that at Ipswich being quite impressive, much of the town centre layout having been updated. The burnished aluminium panels on the trolleybuses were quite unusual but attractive. Colchester was somewhat different, although the variety of chassis and body makers appealed to me. A short visit to the bus station here allowed me to take a few photos of independents but it was to be a few years

Ipswich was one of two municipal operators running only trolleybuses until the 1950s; the other was Darlington. This was one of the 1930 Ipswich all-Ransome single-deckers retained for a route involving a low bridge. One of the new Park Royal-bodied AEC Regent III motorbuses is seen behind.

Following experience of wartime Guy buses, Southampton Corporation continued to specify this make for several years, building up a fleet of 185 double-deckers and 12 underfloor-engined single-deckers, all with Park Royal bodywork. No 180 is seen at the Floating Bridge, then an important terminus before the building of a replacement bridge.

before a further visit allowed me to cover them in more detail.

At Southampton the husband of the lady who ran the guest house was employed on a transatlantic liner, one of which I was to see in the harbour. This reminded me of prewar holidays in Southsea when visitors would stand and admire the British, French and German liners *en route* to Southampton; how times have changed. Unfortunately I was too late to photograph the trams here although I do recall seeing some of them in a scrapyard from the train. The blue livery of earlier years would also have appealed to me

but at least I was in time to see and photograph the prewar Leyland Titans and Cubs together with a return trip on the floating bridge.

In Portsmouth I travelled by trolleybus for a visit to Cosham where I had been told the original fleet of experimental trolleybuses would appear at teatime, but none did. The undertaking had been responsible for promoting my interest in buses on family holidays there in 1937 and 1939 and the comfort and speed of the moquette-seated Craven-bodied AEC 661T trolleybuses was still most impressive. This time I was pleased to see that the ultimate destination was being put to more use than simply showing the prewar

On the opposite side of the river lies Woolston from where Eassons Coaches ran a service to Hedge End on which they operated this Duple-bodied Albion Victor in a cream/brown livery.

Southdown's Hilsea depot forms the background to prewar Leyland Titans of both Portsmouth Corporation and Southdown, carrying Craven and postwar Northern Counties bodies respectively. Both fleets had attractive liveries and were kept in immaculate condition.

'Portsmouth Corporation'. However the old and varied single-deck fleet of prewar had gone, as had the toastracks, but Titans of all ages abounded together with wartime Bedfords and Daimlers.

Another day was similarly spent in Bournemouth but whilst the Southdown fleet seen, but not photographed, had been most interesting, the same could not be said of the standard Tilling monotony of Hants & Dorset which I could just recall in 1939 in its livery of two shades of green and cream. The Bournemouth trolleybus fleet seemed relatively old-fashioned compared to that of Portsmouth but both had updated their overhead although not to my mind

to the same extent as Ispwich at that time. However, Bournemouth appealed to me more as a seaside resort than others visited during the holiday and the two doors of the fleet were unusual but I could see no particular advantage in fitting them.

At Exeter I busied myself in photographing both the Corporation and Devon General fleets. Yes, this time the company did appeal to me, but then the majority of the fleet was AEC! I cannot recall the city being congested, although on subsequent visits it was increasingly so. The Corporation still had prewar Leyland double-deckers in service but these were the Leyland-bodied ones and I was too late to see the

Two consecutively-numbered Portsmouth trolleybuses stand at Cosham. No 301 is a Burlingham-bodied BUT 9611T, then only a few months old, while No 300 is numerically the last of a large batch of tram-replacement Craven-bodied AEC 661Ts built in 1937.

An Exeter Corporation Brush-bodied Daimler CWD6 stands outside St Davids station. Noteworthy are the additional front opening windows and the coat-of-arms on the upper deck panels. Exeter found it necessary to fit additional opening windows to both wartime and several postwar vehicles.

more interesting Craven-bodied examples. The fleet had recently been augmented by a large influx of Daimler CVD6 double-deckers, whose timber-framed Brush bodies must have given as much trouble as the Cravens. The Devon General fleet was quite different, containing many Regal single-deckers of all ages; the postwar Weymann-bodied versions having well proportioned destination boxes giving clear displays.

Arriving in Plymouth for the day I was to receive a shock for whilst I had visited a number of bombed cities, the scene in Plymouth was quite the worst I had seen. It could have been that partially and undamaged buildings had all been demolished to enable the construction of an entirely new centre, but by this date only the main part of the shopping centre and the dual carriageway Royal Parade had been built, leaving a vast area of emptiness. The bombing had also caused considerable damage to the fleet of prewar Titans which had missing roof ventilators and other signs of damage similar to that in

Above:
A smart Weymann-bodied AEC Regent III of Devon General picks up schoolgirls near the Corporation bus depot. In those days vandalism by schoolchildren was virtually non-existent, as was congestion or even parking restrictions in many towns.

A modern dual carriageway now crosses the road where the NAAFI club stood in Plymouth. Servicemen await a bus to Devonport. The Plymouth Corporation Leyland Titan TD4 carries a Weymann-framed body completed by the local firm of Mumford.

Above: **For many years Heybrook Bay Motor Services ran a regular frequency service into Plymouth, latterly from the postwar Bretonside bus station at the opposite end of the city centre to the bomb-flattened surroundings used in 1951. This is a utility Bedford OWB with Duple body.**

Left: **A change of coach at Cheltenham provided the opportunity to photograph a few vehicles, including this dual-purpose Duple-bodied prewar Albion in the original dark red/white livery of Red & White under pre-BTC ownership.**

Sheffield. The fleet had been augmented by a large number of wartime Guys, now resplendent in the new livery of red and cream; together with postwar Crossleys and Leylands, the latest being the first highbridge deliveries following the lowering of the roadway under a low bridge near the city centre.

My return journey to Nottingham on the Sunday was by Associated Motorways operators – Royal Blue and Black & White – via Cheltenham; the one and only time I was to use this interchange. I recall that at Exeter I arrived at the coach two or three minutes before departure and the driver was surprised that a passenger had left it so late. This indicates to me that in those days both drivers and passengers were anxious for a very prompt start. So ended another enjoyable holiday, all spent in dry and often sunny weather, and with more municipals covered. ∎

COVER STORY 2

No 98 in original condition with opening windscreens.

BUILT IN 1958 as part of an order for Trinidad, 889 AAX, along with two similar vehicles, was for some reason not delivered. Eventually these were converted for use in this country, and in 1961 all three were bought by Jones Omnibus Services of Aberbeeg, numbered 98, 99 and 100. Unlike most Tiger Cubs they were fitted with pneumocyclic four-speed gearboxes, hence their nicknames of 'legless buses' or 'Bandits' (the one armed variety). They were repainted from the drab green to the familiar blue/cream of Jones before entering service. Two-speed axles were fitted at a later date as were luggage racks. The windscreens at first had an opening vent, suitable for the hot climate of Trinidad. These were retained at first until mishaps caused them to be replaced by one-piece screens. They gave very little trouble for the whole of their working lives until retirement came in 1975.

A group of Jones' staff decided they would like to preserve one of them, and as No 98 was the best of the trio, it was selected. When taken into the fold of NBC all Jones' vehicles were painted blue, so a repaint was the first task but a lot of other work was done as well. 98 was rallied up and down the country and won many awards, but in 1980 Jones was taken over by Red & White. What with redundancies and having nowhere to store the bus 98 unfortunately had to be sold. It passed to several owners before I purchased it in April 1994.

Having stood idle for many years its condition was rather poor, with faded and peeling paintwork, badly perished window rubbers and the exhaust system shot to pieces. But on connecting the batteries it started at the touch of the button, and ticked over very sweetly indeed. Everything seemed to work alright so I risked the drive from Hampshire to Bristol where it was booked in for its MOT. It failed of course, but at least I then knew what was needed to get it through the next one. In fact it needed a new tyre, new foot valve, complete exhaust system, track rod and adjustment, handbrake linkage and engine mounting. Apart from that it was overheating as I discovered on the way to Bristol.

In June 1994 it passed its MOT and was taken to its first event – the Bristol leisure and motor show. After that I realised that new radiator was the only solution to the overheating problem. As a suitable radiator could not be found a Leopard radiator was cut down to size and using the existing top and bottom tanks the new one was constructed. It's performed perfectly up to now. The next event was the Bristol rally, and it was there that I noticed the fuel tank was leaking slightly.

Attention now was directed to its overall appearance and enquiries were made about finding suitable glazing rubber for the windows. At the same time I started rubbing the vehicle down in preparation for painting. I soon realised that it would take a very long time to complete this task so I took up an offer for a repaint which included rubbing down the rest of it. But first I needed to locate the correct glazing rubber. This took over six months of letters and phone calls to all over

No 98 in later life, in rare NBC blue livery.
Bristol Vintage Bus Group

Britain, but I finally found some in Plymouth. I was told that if I had been a fortnight later it would have been thrown out as they were having a clearout.

I though it would be better to replace the window rubber before painting, so helped by a friend all the windows were taken out one by one and replaced with new rubber. Some of the windows were perspex so new toughened ones were ordered and fitted.It was during this time that the fuel tank was removed for repair.

Pressure was mounting now as spring 1995 was on the way and the first rally was to be at Barry, 98's old territory. I drove it back to Hampshire where the painting was to take place, and a month later collected what looked like a different vehicle. The transformation was incredible. By this time the Tiger Cub badge had been re-chromed and when fittted the bus looked fantastic.

Eight of us travelled the 80 miles to Barry where we received a warm welcome from former Jones employees and ex-passengers alike. Mr Ron Jones, owner of the company, and his son Stuart who took over on Ron's retirement, turned up as well as their families. A photocall was arranged and with three generations of the Jones family in front of the bus the cameras clicked.

It is difficult for anyone who did not know the company to appreciate the esteem in which the

company was held. It may have been small in terms of operating area, but it had a soul!

Several other rallies were attended in 1995 but the most enjoyable outing was when we took it back to Abertillery and Ebbw Vale. We travelled via Gloucester and through the Forest of Dean and Monmouth. The long climb up Blackrock hill to the summit of the Heads of the Valleys road was taken in fourth gear low axle. We even overtook a petrol tanker! We visited the Brecon Mountain Railway where we were met by two former drivers. They directed us to Ebbw Vale where we were allowed to drive through the now-pedestrianised shopping area. We parked outside the police station where many passers-by expressed delight and surprise at our presence. We then followed some of the old routes through Cwm, Six Bells and Abertillery, not forgetting the old Jones' garage at Aberbeeg.

I have enjoyed my first year of ownership. Not only the rallies and road runs, but working on the bus, improving its looks and getting everything working properly. There is a long way to go yet, but eventually everything will, I hope, be done. ■

BRISTOLS OF CHRISTCHURCH

Almost a UK bus – Christchurch Bristol RELL6L No 468 with ECW/Hawke 47-seat body. Painted in the 1978-introduced red/white livery, with ECW grey window rubbers, it is almost a classic Lowestoft product.

Frank Rowlands

The classic Bristol RE was not just a home market model, as FRANK ROWLANDS recalls

BUS OPERATORS in New Zealand have traditionally obtained their fleets – or at least, the chassis for those fleets – from Britain. Some inroads were made by American designs, but among the most important sources were AEC, Leyland, Bedford, BUT and Bristol. The Christchurch Transport Board, biggest Council public-transit providers in the South Island, maintained an impressive roster of RELL6L buses between 1974 and 1990. Thereafter the ECW-style vehicles were phased out, and by 1992 the only REs left in service were the newest, repowered with MAN engines.

These 21 buses carry unusual Hess-type welded-aluminium bodies erected under licence in New Zealand by New Zealand Motor Bodies. Nos 578/80-99, were the last to remain in City ownership out of a total of 96 similar vehicles built from 1978 to 1981. Several of the older machines have been sold to private operators. The Hess is a visually-impressive beast, and ultra-modern at the time of its introduction. Even today, they are of sleeker appearance than the boxy MAN SL202s, which are somewhat newer!

All Bristol REs run by the Board (incidentally, the only REs in New Zealand) had Leyland 510 engines. These units were rated at 150hp and set up to provide plenty of torque at low revs. As delivered, each bus was fitted with a four-speed semi-automatic gearbox (CAV design) which enabled the vehicle to attain a maximum speed of about 50mph under ideal conditions. During most city runs, drivers were required to keep their velocity well down, but some of the country routes to outlying suburbs and towns were a good excuse for bursts of high speed. With this in mind, and with a view to capturing some of the lucrative charter market, the CTB converted transmissions in nine of the Hess Bristols to five-speed standard. Nos 600-8 became genuine 'flyers' after this change, well-liked by drivers because of their ability to maintain 60mph for long periods out on the open road. In addition to this mechanical alteration,the Board also rebuilt No 608 to single-door format and installed special high-backed seating. This bus was then treated as a dedicated sightseeing and luxury-charter vehicle. Upon withdrawal in 1991, No 608 found a job carting excursionists to a remote resort area, then subsequently was sold again, this time to the operator who took over the City-to-Airport service in Christchurch.

It is perhaps unfortunate that few of the special transmissions have survived; most were replaced with conventional assemblies. This backward step seems to have characterised the bus scene here for a long time. Technological and operational advances are made, then largely nullified by subsequent actions in the relentless pursuit of so-called progress! The derating of the CTB's first AEC Swift, and the introduction of 'deregulated competitive service tendering' are two prime examples – but these are stories for another time.

When the first Bristols arrived it was evident that, although their leaf-spring suspension could not offer the quality of ride possible in the early-1950s AEC Regal MkIVs and the 1971 AEC Swift, the wide doors, low steps, large windows and comfortable seating put them into a new and high class of public transport vehicle. All of the REs were fitted with 46 passenger seats, with a generous amount of leg room between each row. The plentiful handrails added to an overall impression of solidenss and safety. Clearly, this batch

of 25 buses represented something up-to-date and long overdue for the travellers of Christchurch. A second series of REs, with New Zealand-built bodywork, came along in 1977 and 1978. These buses were significantly different to the ECW-based vehicles of 1974-75.

The 'MkII' Bristols (fleet Nos 484-512) were of generally similar appearance to the earlier batch, but in detail could not be confused with the ECW design. One of the most noticeable changes was in body profile. The new bodies had curved-in sides below the waistrail, which continued on a constant radius down to the bottom of the skirt; the ECW type was straight and vertical from waistrail to a few inches above the bottom edge, then sharply curved under. This distinctive difference made the MkI buses look somewhat more stylish and solid than the later machines.

Other design changes for the second batch were many and varied. The New Zealand-built bodies (as opposed to knocked-down ECW sections assembled locally) were formed of steel, not alloy. Consequently, the new buses were heavier than the ECWs by about 8cwt. Even the style of the waistrail was different – flat, not curved. The opening toplights in the saloon windows were deeper, and all of the sliding type, rather than some being pull-ins. The bumper design was made more substanial, the grille mesh and mounting got altered, as did the position for the windscreen wiper shafts. Significantly, the design of the front lamp cluseter was revised to a simpler, but older, style.

All of the MkI Bristols carried front lamp assemblies made for the Leyland National. British readers will no doubt be well aware of the modernistic appearance of the National, due in no small part to the inspired combination of headlight, sidelight, and indicator lenses into one close group. It was this feature which really emphasised the 'modular' nature of the new Leyland. Placing this attractive cluster onto a traditional ECW RELL nose enhanced the product by taking the bus into the 1970s; it was a cunning disguise of an old form.

Regrettably, the Christchurch Transport Board replaced these clusters with conventional headlights and separate indicators, over a period of a few years. Motivated by expediency rather than whim, the fleet managers realised that their Board would not be keen

to pay for expensive, imported replacement parts to repair damaged units, so they opted for a cost-effective alternative supply.

There are a lot of noteworthy aspects to the RELL story in New Aealand, some of which are scanned in this brief survey. In terms of the public's perception of these buses, it would be fair to say that the advent of overall advertising liveries in the 1970s had a big impact upon the bus scene and its relationship to the fare-paying passenger or casual observer. First tried on the 1958 AEC Reliances, colours and slogans other than the 'proper' CTB scheme soon ran riot through the fleet.

Being very long buses, the Bristols were eminently suitable for carrying liveries calculated to produce maximum visual registration. The once-uniform fleet of reds was turned into an assortment or greens, yellows, purples, whites, and – even worse, from the purists' point of view – 'variegateds', sporting several hues. Some of these special buses (all of which continued in everyday route service) were so multicoloured and/or gaudy that they actually blended into a background of shops. The eye was initially fooled, rather than shocked or impressed.

In wrapping up my tale, mention should be made of the many Bristols that passed out of Council ownership. The Board was replaced by a profit-driven local authority enterprise in 1990/1, becoming Christchurch Transport Ltd. There was to be no place in the new competitive era for British buses. It is fortunate that a MkI, a MkII and a 'Hess' have passed into active preservation with the trend-setting Tramway Historical Society; Nos 480, 510 and 538 were generously gifted to that body. Several of the MkII vehicles, and some of the 'Hess' type, were sold to small commercial operators.

Following New Zealand custom, a few Bristols have been rebuilt by private individuals into motor caravans. However, it is very sad that No 475 (originally No 457) the first of the breed did not go into preservation. As of 1995, this historic bus is still in existence, but derelict, and with an unhappy future. As an enthusiast of the RE, I can only hope that this article provokes British bus fans into securing a place in mainstream history for what was a fine, if misunderstood, example of engineering. ■

TWILIGHT SHIFT

S J BUTLER dipped into his collection to illustrate some buses and coaches in use on non-psv duties

Above: **Two utility Guy Arabs with lowered roofs in Grassington Square in 1960. The vehicle on the left was new to London Transport, the vehicle on the right to Crosville.**

Left: **Building contractors have regularly used old buses for transport to and from sites, and Tarmac was using this ex-North Western 1946 Bristol L5G with 35-seat ECW bodywork.**

A fine vehicle for a contractor – a 1952 Leyland Royal Tiger PSU1/15/Harrington from the Southdown extended tours fleet in use by Wimpey at Enfield.

This bus, used by McAlpine at Wigan, was new as a demonstrator for the Leyland/MCW Olympian LW44 – an integral version of the Tiger Cub. After use as a demonstrator it passed to Jones of Aberbeeg.

This East Kent Dennis Lancet II with 35-seat Park Royal rear entrance coach body was new to East Kent and was sold in 1963 to Fell, Wakefield. It was withdrawn by the contractor two years later.

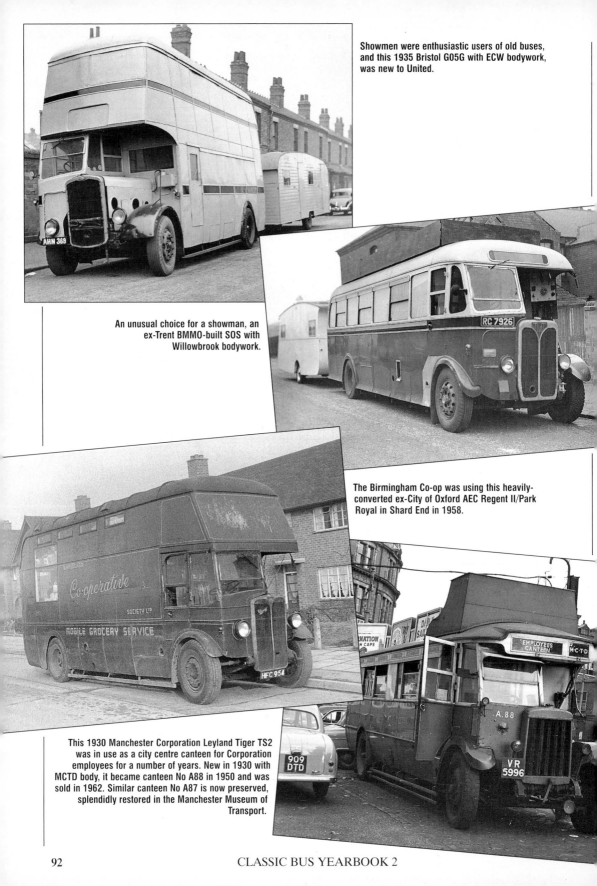

Showmen were enthusiastic users of old buses, and this 1935 Bristol G05G with ECW bodywork, was new to United.

An unusual choice for a showman, an ex-Trent BMMO-built SOS with Willowbrook bodywork.

The Birmingham Co-op was using this heavily-converted ex-City of Oxford AEC Regent II/Park Royal in Shard End in 1958.

This 1930 Manchester Corporation Leyland Tiger TS2 was in use as a city centre canteen for Corporation employees for a number of years. New in 1930 with MCTD body, it became canteen No A88 in 1950 and was sold in 1962. Similar canteen No A87 is now preserved, splendidly restored in the Manchester Museum of Transport.

Cleethorpes Corporation received two Roe 43-seat D650HS Freeline buses in 1953/5. MFU 678 was the later one, chassis 25542, and given the interest in internal design experimentation at the time, was a little unusual among Freelines in being a conventionally-seated one-door bus.

R F Mack

THE FREEDOM FACTOR

DAVID STANIER remembers Daimler's underfloor engined chassis for the 1950s – the Freeline

THE OFFICIAL literature for the Daimler Freeline declares that this new chassis 'permits absolute freedom in body design and construction, providing maximum seating capacity and all types and positions of entrances and exits' – this rather wordy advertising tended to disguise the fact that the maximum length for single-deck psvs had recently been increased to 30ft, and so it was now possible to contemplate 41 seats for coach use and up to 45 for service bus use. The overseas market also tended to specify high-capacity vehicles for their general operations.

Daimler followed others into the underfloor-engined philosophy. During the early postwar years, BMMO,

AEC and Leyland had all made significant progress within this configuration. It was not until 1950 that Daimler chose to enter this sector of the market, but not without thoroughly testing the idea first.

A pair of 19ft wheelbase CV-derived chassis (longer than standard wheelbase length) were laid down in 1950 solely for the experimental application of horizontally-mounted engines. The engines used were Daimler's own 10.62 litre unit (used in the robust CD650 chassis since 1948) and the Gardner 6HLW 8.4 litre engine (used vertically-mounted in Daimler products since the mid 1930s in the COG6 and later CVG6 models). In horizontal form, the Daimler engine was known as the D650H and developed either 140 or 150bhp at 1800/2000rpm respectively. The less-powerful Gardner engine developed 112bhp at 1700rpm, and was therefore more likely to suit bus users rather than the coaching sector.

The two test-beds, coded CD6F and CG6F according to engine type, were never intended for

Some 85% of Freeline production was sold to export customers. This 17ft 6in wheelbase left-hand drive chassis may well be one of the later examples, as it has only two-pedal control with semi-automatic selector, and a rear-mounted spare wheel. The three same-sided fillers and weight-saving holes in the chassis members are clearly shown. *Daimler*

The original Freeline S650HS chassis, 25000, was built in 1951 and fitted with Burlingham Seagull 37-seat coachwork. This style of body was ultimately the most popular choice among UK operators – 23 were supplied. The registration LKV 218 was allocated in 1952. The fluted Daimler badge, pre-empting Fleetline models a decade later, was mounted on the access to the spare wheel.

Daimler

bodying. They covered considerable mileage in chassis form, boasting their identity with chromed CV-style radiators and 'Daimler' names on the ballast boxes. They must have been fun to drive (except perhaps in wet weather!).

Old-fashioned halfcab single-deckers continued into the 30ft era in very limited numbers. Some front-engined models took on fully-fronted body styles in some cases, but the underfloor-engined vehicles soon made even these look outdated. Nevertheless, Daimler kept the CV-series single-deckers in production until 1955.

So in 1951 the chassis was launched as the Freeline – Daimler broke with tradition in naming the chassis in this way. Daimler's general chassis numbering was around 19xxx at the time, but a new series reserved for

the Freeline leapt forward to 25000. The general chassis number series continued for other Daimler products until 1968 (by which time, other specially-allocated series were also in use, for example Fleetline and Roadliner production).

The Freeline chassis designations were apparently D650HS and G6HS although none of the official literature seen by the writer refers to these (perhaps the company chassis record only uses this coding). It is also reported that some chassis plates fixed to vehicles carried D650SD and G6HSD!

The first Freeline chassis comprised a Daimler-engined type fitted with Burlingham Seagull 37-seat bodywork. This proved to be the most common body style for those specified by British coach operators in due course. The original one remained unregistered

The prototype Freeline G6HS, chassis 25001, was exhibited at the 1951 Scottish Motor Show. It carried Duple bodywork seating 36, with standee space. The dual-door (rear entrance) configuration was initially tried out by Edinburgh Corporation alongside experimental standee buses from Leyland, a Royal Tiger and an Olympic, at the instigation of transport manager Moris Little. LRW 377 remained in Edinburgh for a year or so, but is seen here later in its demonstration career (which lasted until 1956) on loan to West Bromwich Corporation. The absence of opening windows is of interest. It still wears Edinburgh madder/white livery, though it has lost its temporary fleetnumber, 800.

Roy Marshall

for a time, and featured in publicity and technical literature. A Gardner-engined example was fitted with 36-seat bus style bodywork by Duple, this vehicle featuring the unusual arrangement of front exit and rear entrance! The latter vehicle was given Edinburgh Corporation livery and shown at the 1951 Scottish Motor Show. Both these Freelines acted as demonstrators for some time, being registered LKV 218 and LRW 377 respectively in spring 1952 and autumn 1951.

A third 1951-built Freeline remained as an unbodied chassis, and so this would amply show the technical features to full advantage. In typical Daimler manner, the Freeline employed a preselector/fluid flywheel transmission to afford smooth gearchanging, reducing maintenance and extending gearbox life; four or five-speed options were available, the former generally being more suitable for service bus operation. The braking system was based on hydraulics, as with the CD650, but power steering was not generally fitted, being offered as an option on long wheelbase models for export. Home customers were confined to the 16ft 4in wheelbase version, whereas 17ft 6in (33ft overall length) and 20ft 4in (35ft overall length) models were available for overseas customers. The latter would allow up to 64 passenger capacity given 3+2 seating. In fact, the longest specification was chosen by one South African customer only.

Other chassis features designed to assist with maintenance schedules included the fitting of fillers down one side only, with battery access through the floor traps and access to the spare wheel from the front of the chassis. Weight distribution was evenly spread and chassis suspension was equally loaded between axles.

Hill climbing

The Freeline was a good hill-climber, had a tight turning circle and good, smooth acceleration. It was expected to return an average fuel consumption of 14mpg, but I have no operator evidence to support this in reality. The five-speed coaches could achieve 50-55mph as a top speed fairly comfortably, which in those days was quite impressive.

Underfloor-engined vehicles always had the disadvantage of presenting a high floor and numerous steps for passengers. The Freeline was every bit as bad in this respect, and combined with the heavily-engineered chassis specification (which one has to remember followed hard on the heels of the CD650, which some found rather too much to contemplate!) probably formed the basis of the slow reception it had in the UK market. However, the tendency to cool running was a good selling point in those parts of the world with warmer climates and proved to be in the favour of the model.

In Britain, only five operators took the Freeline as a service bus, accounting for just 16 vehicles (and 50% of these were built right at the end of the production run). Overseas though, it was a different story, as most were used as service buses rather than coaches.

Above: Gash of Newark had built up a fleet of Daimler CVD6s in the postwar boom years and it was not surprising to find that the company had ordered two early D650HS Freelines, chassis 25004/5. NAL 783, new in 1952 with Burlingham Seagull bodywork, is seen in the London area.
R H G Simpson

Below: One of the more unusual bodybuilders to handle Freelines was Heaver of Durrington. KWP 27, chassis 25008, was the first of just two, this one new in 1952 to Johnson of Stourbridge, though seen later with Bryn Melyn Motor Services of Llangollen. The fluted badge, usually fitted on new-look CVG6 cowls, was unusual on a Freeline.
C Cressey collection

Above: **Unique among Freelines was this 1952 Harrington-bodied D650HS for Kitchin & Sons of Pudsey, LWT 704, chassis 25178. The characteristic dorsal fin was fitted as with other Harrington products of the time.**
J R Neale collection

Below: **SHMD Board No 67 (PLG 967) was shown at the 1952 Commercial Motor Show, and generated much interest. Experiments with standee buses continued, and in conjunction with SHMD, Northern Counties produced this unusual 60-passenger (including 26 standing) body. Twin power-operated doors were mounted on the centre nearside. PLG 967 (chassis 25214) was the first G6HS Freeline built to the order of a UK customer.**

British coach operators seemed to stutter over the Freeline. One went here, another two there, another one here . . . and so it went on! During 1952-3, only 43 Freeline coaches entered service in this country, and what must have been even more disappointing for Daimler was that some 29 more were cancelled during these early years of production – these were generally one or two-off requirements. Matters were worse in 1954-5, for only 28 coaches were sold to British operators. The Freeline had already had its day!

The export market was certainly more encouraging. The first models to go overseas were G6HS examples for South Africa and two fitted with Gardner five-cylinder engines for Bombay, India, in 1952. The 7.0 litre 5HLW Gardner engine (always listed as an option) produced 94bhp at 1200rpm, and although not published officially, is taken as being designated G5HS.

By 1954, the Freeline was into Australia, New Zealand (the first quantity order), Gold Coast (later Ghana) in Africa, Belgium, Norway and some more G5HS models had gone to India. In all, some 300 units had been sold abroad by this time.

The next four years saw reduced, but steady trade to foreign customers, with new representation in Portugal, Spain and Israel. About 275 units were built for export in this period.

The last Freelines

The British demand for the Freeline had ended to all intents and purposes after 1955 deliveries had been

Mann Egerton 50-seat half-decker bodywork was fitted to this D650HS chassis, 25015, new in 1953 to Don Everall, Wolverhampton

Daimler

completed. Curiously, a little ember re-kindled in 1958-59 (by this time, export customers had more of less gone away too!) accounting for the final Daimler-engined models for British users, while in 1960, the very last D650HS models went to Portugal and South Africa. As stated earlier, the final eight Freelines, all G6HS models, were built for home use in 1962/4, these having specially lowered driving positions. Only 25 Freelines were built between 1959 and 1964!

Only eight British coach users took more than two Freelines into their fleets, the largest being Blue Cars of London which had eight. The other 'quantity' users were Don Everall, Wolverhampton; Red House Motor Services, Coventry; Burwell & District; Cronshaw, London; Pyne, Harrogate; Central, Walsall and finally, Coventry Corporation.

One can only speculate why the Freeline was such a lemon in the eyes of the British operators. Firstly, others got there first, albeit with less sophisticated specifications. Secondly, the Freeline was a 'heavy old slug', which in spite of publicity expectations, would have impacted into fuel consumption (at a time when the Suez troubles affected supply); others had lighter-weight models in production, although to be fair to

A left-hand drive 17ft 6in Freeline for Belgium, in Belgian Railways colours, with Van Hool two door body with seats for 36 and standing space for a further 34.

Daimler

Another standee experiment was this early D650HS experimental chassis, 25003, bodied in 1953 by Alexander for Glasgow Corporation. The centre entrance body had seats for 32, inward-facing in the rear portion and single seats opposite the wide door.

Daimler

Five per cent of Freelines were exported to Australia. This is a G6HS chassis, 25055, for MTT, Adelaide, new in 1953. It was bodied in Australia by Lawton, and was probably built as a 40-seater.

J Bull

JDN 712 (chassis 25250) was a D650HS service bus for Reliance Motors of York. Built in 1954, the Duple bodywork was similar to that on LRW 377 except that it was single entrance and had opening ventilators.

Michael Dryhurst collection

Duple Elizabethan bodywork was introduced in 1954 and is seen here on RVM 37, chassis 25016, of 1955, in use with Stevensons of Spath during the late 1960s. It was new to North Manchester Coaches and was fitted with 41 seats.

P J Relf

The only G6HS coaches for British operation were three Willowbrook-bodied models built for Coventry Corporation towards the end of the Freeline production run, in 1959. The trio, chassis 25710-2, were 41-seaters and sported Fleetline-style fluted badges.

UVE 101 of June 1959 may have been the final D650HS delivered to a UK operator – vying for the title with Blue Bus Services 120 JRB. It was a Plaxton Panorama for Burwell & District, chassis 25713.

D J Stanier collection

The very last Freeline, chassis 25726: Great Yarmouth No 20 showed some signs of the new era in bus styling, with a one-piece windscreen and larger glazed sections in the entrance doors. Year-suffix registrations were also allocated to the final three Freelines. As one Daimler single-decker bowed out, another made its debut later in 1964 – the Roadliner!

J R Neale

Daimler, efforts at weight reduction were made in the chassis design and construction. Thirdly, the caution which operators demonstrated towards hydraulic braking systems must have been a problem.

At the time the Freeline was delisted, the 36ft length limit for single-deckers was in place, and Daimler certainly did not lag behind the others in developing its model to these dimensions- incorporating a rear engine as well. By this time, the big D650H engine had gone and the company opted for further development on the 8.6 litre CD6 engine instead. This found its way into a 36ft chassis in 1960.

Unfortunately, Daimler ceased building diesel engines for its commercial chassis soon afterwards, and the forthcoming Roadliner single-decker went on to become another lemon, selling fewer than half the number of Freeline chassis.

The Freeline was not a failure though – that would be too much to bear! D650HS-powered Freelines served well in New Zealand at least for more than 20 years!

My own direct experience of the Freeline model was with chassis 25709, 120 JRB, which came very late in the course of production. 'Eighteen', as the Blue Bus staff called her, was a 'weighty old tub', being almost as heavy as a CD650 double-decker! It had air assisted gear-change, so that a loud hiss could be heard whenever the gear selector pedal was depressed. It could run at about 55mph as a top speed, and perhaps the only drawback was the rattly nature of bodywork fittings towards the end of its service career in 1973. ■

I must express my thanks to Michael Dryhurst, who kindly suggested I should prepare this article, and besides some photographic submissions from him too, other photographs were submitted by Jim Neale of Burwell, Colin Cressey of Portishead, Terry Middleton of Burton on Trent and John Ashmore of West Wittering. I also must acknowledge the PSV Circle records covering Daimler Freeline chassis, and the published works of Alan Townsin and Stewart J Brown.

DAIMLER FREELINE – EXPORT SALES

Country \ Year	1952	1953	1954	1955	1956	1957	1958	1960	Total
Australia	–	3	2	4	1	18	5	–	33
Belgium	–	17	–	8	3	–	1	–	29
Gold Coast (Ghana)	–	3	14	–	–	–	–	–	17
India	2	–	20	–	–	–	–	–	22
Israel	–	–	–	–	–	–	20	–	20
New Zealand	–	46	53	3	48	9	12	–	171
Nigeria	–	–	–	–	–	16	6	–	22
Norway	–	29	–	19	–	–	–	–	48
Portugal	–	–	–	8	7	7	4	1	27
South Africa	1	15	64	22	30	22	–	10	164
Spain	–	–	–	–	–	1	1	–	2
USSR (Trade Delegation)	–	–	–	–	–	1	–	–	1
Total	3	113	153	64	89	74	49	11	556

N.B. No Freelines were exported in 1951/9/61–4

DAIMLER FREELINE – CHASSIS PRODUCTION SUMMARY

		1951	1952	1953	1954	1955	1956	1957	1958	1959	1960	1961	1962	1963	1964	Total
D650H	Export –		–	100	80	61	89	58	43	–	11	–	–	–	–	442
	UK Chassis only	1	2	–	–	–	–	–	–	–	–	–	–	–	–	3
	UK Coach	1	16	27	4	14	–	–	1	3	–	–	–	–	–	66
	UK Dual purpose	–	1	–	–	–	–	–	–	–	–	–	–	–	–	1
	UK Bus	–	–	3	5	1	–	–	–	–	–	–	–	–	–	9
G6HS	Export –			1	13	53	3	–	16	6	–	–	–	–	–	–	92
	UK Chassis only	–	–	–	–	–	–	–	–	–	–	–	–	–	–	–
	UK Coach	–	–	–	–	–	–	–	–	3	–	–	–	–	–	3
	UK Dual purpose	–	–	–	–	–	–	–	–	–	–	–	5	–	3	8
	UK Bus	1	–	1	–	–	–	–	–	–	–	–	–	–	–	2
G5HS	Export	–	2	–	20	–	–	–	–	–	–	–	–	–	–	22
TOTAL		3	22	144	162	79	89	74	50	6	11	–	5	–	3	648

COVER STORY

The neat lines of the little Croft body on the preserved Thornycroft. Note the traditional MacBrayne clansman symbol.

Photos by Derek Hunter

Extensive body damage on the Maudslay meant that expensive repairs had to be made before it could be restored to its former glory. The back end was a particular problem. The wording in the rear glass read 'Royal Mail Services'.

THE NAME David MacBrayne conjures up romantic memories of small buses sitting on sun-dappled island piers awaiting the steamer from the Scottish mainland, and of trunk coach services linking Glasgow with the majesty of the highlands. And for many people in Scotland's highlands and islands David MacBrayne was the main link with the rest of the world.

David MacBrayne was the man involved in West Highland shipping services in the 19th century, and in 1906 the company that carried his name started its first motorbus service. The motor side of the business – buses and lorries – continued to grow, with AECs and Bedfords particularly favoured. For a short period in the early postwar years MacBrayne bought Commers, Maudslays and Thornycrofts, but returned to AECs and Bedfords in 1952. After control of the company passed to the newly-formed Scottish Transport Group in 1968/9, the bus operations were passed over to neighbouring STG companies, Highland Omnibuses and Western SMT. The last MacBrayne bus service ran early in 1973.

Many will remember MacBrayne's vehicles from holidays in Scotland, and that was how Derek Hunter came to know them. As a youngester he holidayed in Ardrishaig, and he is now the proud owner of three MacBrayne vehicles – very tangible souvenirs of holidays past.

The two that feature on the back cover date from 1949/50.

On the left is HGG 359, a Thornycroft Nippy HF/ER4 with Glasgow-built Croft 20-seat bus body, new in July 1950 and one of six bought that year. No 149 was based at Ardrishaig at one time, and also worked on Islay. When it was withdrawn in 1962 it passed to another operator, MacLachlan of Tayvallich, who sold it to preservationist Alan Nightingale in 1974.

Derek Hunter went to Farnborough to see the bus in 1991 and ended up buying it. He collected it on a low-loader and brought it back to Fordoun, near Stonehaven, where he runs a road haulage business. A joiner rebuilt the roof, the worst part of the body structure, and it was finished off by Robin Gloag at Errol. The engine was rebuilt. 'It didn't need a lot of work', says Derek. 'It was still in pretty good nick.'

Today it is regularly rallied in Scotland, often on its old stamping-grounds.

Alongside the Thornycroft on the back cover is GUS 926, No 136, a Maudslay Marathon III with 35-seat Park Royal body, one of 16 bought in 1949. The Maudslays were front-line MacBrayne coaches for some years and were to be found on services to Fort William, Kinlochleven and Ardrishaig. No 136 ended up in Inverness, and it was kept on after the others had gone because, says Derek, 'someone had an affection for it'. Withdrawn in 1966, it was sold to a Dundee showman, then in 1971 passed to the Albion Vehicle Preservation Trust. After eight years it passed on to vintage coach operator David Deans of Paisley, and then found its way to South Wales and Derek Hunter bought it from there in 1992.

'It was in a sorry state when we got it', he says. 'There was a lot of costly body work to do. Fortunately most bits were there, so we reassembled them. We retrimmed the seats and the ceiling.'

The Thornycroft and the Maudslay are not Derek's only MacBrayne vehicles. He also has 198 CUS, a 1961 AEC Reliance with Duple Midland 41-seat body; this bus passed to Highland Omnibuses in October 1970 with the Ardrishaig and Oban area services, and was withdrawn in 1977. Derek Hunter has had this bus since 1981 and early in 1996 it was being completely refurbished internally.

For a relatively small fleet, there is a good selection of postwar MacBrayne vehicles in preservation. In addition to Derek's three, other members of The MacBrayne Circle own various types of AEC and Bedford, and there are known to be others. ∎

Timpson's AEC Regal at Eccleston Bridge, Victoria. The London-Margate-Broadstairs-Ramsgate service ran several times daily in the summer, and also on a reduced frequency for the rest of the year at one time. Eccleston Bridge was used by several coach service operators, including Green Line, as a picking-up point or terminus, but Timpson's only came here after sampling several other points nearby. Under BET/Tilling control the company moved again, to nearby Victoria Coach Station.

COACH TO THE COAST

with all seats numbered and reserved?

JOHN DUNABIN
remembers coach services from London between the Wars

THIS WILL smack of heresy or at least be quite incomprehensible to some of my London-born friends, for whom the lure of the motorbus, intense in Piccadilly Circus or outside Victoria station, fades as soon as they leave the Metropolis. To me however the London bus scene, when I first became familiar with it over 60 years ago, seemed rather dull, hardly anything but AECs and all in a rather washed-out red and white livery.

Perhaps it was a reaction bred of disappointment at not having got there a couple of years earlier, before LT uniformity had been imposed; this was probably exacerbated by hints here and there of what had been lost, such as rounded outlines (ex-Thomas Tilling) on the 12 and the 36. At a more practical level there were open staircases, and even, to my amazement, solid tyres. On the 69, observed during peak hours when it was extended south from Camberwell Green to Herne Hill, both seemed standard.

What is more, I quickly found that buses in London could be, regularly were, full; walking south over the temporary Waterloo Bridge or resorting to packed trains were the only sensible ways to get home. And when it came to pleasure travel the tramcar with its bargain fares, 2d 'mid-day' all the way from the Embankment to Abbey Wood, 6d in the evenings anywhere south of the river plus the Embankment and a few stubs, or if time justified the extra outlay one shilling all day in the County of London, was the obvious choice.

What brightened the scene, apart from Victoria Coach Station with its riot of colour, were the coaches of the London-based seasonal operators, Blue Belle, King's Emerald, Grey Coaches, Orange Luxury,

Small beginnings: a garage view of a Chevrolet in the Emerald fleet of W King & Sons Ltd.

All photos from the J F Higham collection

Timpsons (cream with maroon lining and the name in large Gothic lettering), Venture of Hendon in yellow and black, and United Service Transport in a handsome dark green which also appeared in the omnipresent van fleet delivering one of London's evening newspapers. There were many others too, all with well-kept vehicles, but those of Timpsons and United Service stood out as immaculate. Strangely, their activities seem to have been overlooked by the chroniclers, with one or two exceptions.

The development of regular long distance coach services to and from London, starting in earnest in 1925, was powered essentially from outside, as were earlier seasonal and/or weekend services by Chapmans from Eastbourne, Royal Blue from Bournemouth and Southdown Motor Services, largely by independents. The regional bus companies took part in some cases on their own initiative – those in Kent and Sussex were already involved in a minor way – and then by purchase, until by the middle to late 1930s their control of this market, apart from a 'hole' in Essex/Suffolk, was almost complete.

Magnet

Most of their business appeared to be provincially generated, with London as the magnet. Some of the early services did not reach central London at all; it is difficult to imagine many residents of say East Ham or Dartford, despite extensive publicity, finding their way to Hammersmith for coaches to the West Country.

Alongside them however, and starting inconspicuously some years earlier without a great deal of overlap, was another very large group of providers who grew up to cater for a different market, with cheap bucket-and-spade trips to the seaside, by charabanc of course at first, no covered tops here! Theirs was a very seasonal business, peaking in July/August, but the demand was enormous, siphoning

off and adding greatly to the excursion traffic developed earlier by the railways. A pioneering London-Brighton service started in August 1905 by the London Motor Omnibus Co ('Vanguard') and continuing through the winter, ended in disaster on 12 July 1906 when, following mechanical failure, the Milnes Daimler employed, carrying a private party from Orpington over the route, crashed on Handcross Hill with the loss of 10 lives and many injuries. This accident deterred emulators for over a decade, but like the sinking of the Titanic later, it was now past history and largely forgotten.

Within a few years a partial separation of this group, partial and never complete, arose between the smaller number of operators whose main aim was to take up traffic from Central London, daily all-the-year-round where demand justified, and those whose target was the native millions living further out who rarely if ever visited the West End. The former included Cambrian, Cornells, Samuelsons, and Mr L M Turnham. Significantly perhaps the first three, attempting to serve a range of seaside resorts, did not survive, but Mr Turnham, who started with a London-Brighton service in conjunction with Pickfords, also early in this field, went on to form London Coastal Coaches. This organisation gathered under its wing almost all the major regional companies running long distance services into London, with one or two independents, notably West London Coaches and later South Midland. A very early participant, surprisingly, was Edward Paul of Forest Hill, a seasonal operator and surely a misfit. Edward Paul Ltd, it should be added, was also, starting in 1923, a London bus operator.

This left out some emergent giants, some embryo giants, and numerous others whose combined catchment areas stretching out to Hatfield, Kingston-upon-Thames, Watford, Waltham Abbey, Ilford, Croydon, Sutton and beyond.

Again there was some separation, starting early, but again it was not clear-cut. Some of them spread widely, with quite a number of picking-up points in the London area and eventually running to or through as many as 20 seaside towns ranging from Great Yarmouth to Torquay. Most concentrated on a fairly early morning outward journey and an evening return (earlier on Saturdays) except for Torquay; the one-way trip took all day. A few targeted one main route, eg MT to Thanet, one of the first, Monty to Clacton and a bit beyond, Golden West to Bournemouth, Empire's Best, also to Clacton but by a unique route, and Carrimore to Southend. Eclipse (Neal) of Acton had two services, one to Clacton and the other to Yarmouth. Some of these services became all-the-year-round operations, those of MT and Empire's Best being two, with several daily timings and intermediate fares, and when pressures mounted on the seasonal operators from various quarters such providers felt they deserved special treatment, but they were damned by association. Mr F A Flin, partner in the pioneering MT business, fought very determinedly, but only just managed to prevent the Traffic Commissioners from giving too much of his business away to East Kent. The official view was that the regional bus companies needed the cream to enrich the skimmed milk of their essential but less profitable local services.

George Ewer Ltd (Grey-Green), still in 1930 essentially a London seasonal business, managed to retain, at least from Kings Cross outwards, its frequent London-Felixstowe service, adding to this until the company became, in postwar years, a major all-the-year-round operator, spreading far and wide over the country.

More flexible arrangements

Going back a little in time, it all began with days out (excursions), with an early morning start and a middle to late evening return, but demands later arose for more flexible arrangements as regards both times and fares. Most interesting was the spreading into what might be called the 'London Coastal' type services. Together with the Felixstowe one and others mentioned above, these included a three times daily run between London and Brighton via Epsom, with over 40 intermediate timing points, including several in central London, and short distance fares such as London-Leatherhead, run by United Service Transport. Another one of the same company had seven daily journeys, also to Brighton, but running via Reigate. A similar service to Portsmouth and Southsea had apparently been withdrawn before the end of 1931. Timpsons ran from Central London to Sheerness with intermediate timings four or five times each day, and several times daily to Brighton, Ramsgate and

Top: **An Albion Valiant in the Emerald fleet, seen parked near Kings Cross. Kings used the coach station in Euston Road as its principal London terminus.**

Above: **Very different from the Grey-Green image of later days. This is a Thornycroft Dainty.**

Hastings. The Hastings service, believed to be Timpsons' earliest, was strongly established, aided no doubt by public awareness of the Timpson name; the company also provided a network of local services in and around the town, competing with the trams and later trolleybuses of the Hastings Tramways Co.

A London-Folkestone-Dover-Deal-Sandwich Timpson service of 1931 clearly catered essentially for reverse direction passengers, with a morning (8am) inward and an evening (M-F) outward journey plus an earlier Saturday return. Was this perhaps the first commuter coach service?

Orange Luxury had morning and evening journeys from both ends on its London-Dover-Deal and London-Ashford-Hythe-Folkestone routes, but the most frequent Orange service was the one to Brighton,

Perhaps one of the ugliest-looking coaches of the time – a Karrier of C G Lewis, Greenwich.

Luggage accommodation was most important for holidaymakers, but for a long time it had to be stowed on the roof. How it got there is evident from this view of an Eastern Belle Maudslay ML4 – note the slightly superfluous running-board.

running seven times daily with the last outward departure at 11.30pm. In fact, the total number of timetabled Brighton departures by the principal 'seasonal' operators, including Langs and Grey Coaches, amounted at its peak to 25 against Southdown's 11, but of course they had no common central picking-up point. While this may have been partly a reflection of their independence, it was undoubtedly influenced by Metropolitan Police views on street congestion.

Returning to the broader picture, with few exceptions no intermediate fares were available, this permitting shorter actual journey times, but the situation regarding picking-up points was very different. There were, including what might be described as occasional providers, some hundreds of coastally-orientated London coachmen, with at the peak, timetabled pick-ups which must have run into four figures, some of the larger operators serving 50 or more on a daily basis. There was considerable overlapping, focal points such as Camberwell Green, Islington, Lewisham, Stratford and Woolwich for

example each having several of them competing for custom. Nearer to the centre, Kings Cross, Victoria (not the coach station of course), Westbourne Grove and even the Embankment had several operators calling there. The Terminal Station in Clapham Road, which was later to become Blue Belle's headquarters (with 'foreigners' then relegated to the open forecourt), was also popular.

There was some bunching of operating bases too. In Plumstead there were two running side by side, Bradshaws and Buckleys, in Croydon two, John Bennett and Bourne & Balmer, two sizeable ones in Hendon, Cronshaws and Venture, etc, while in Stockwell two of the larger ones, Blue Belle and United Service, were cheek by jowl with Orange Luxury not far away.

Co-operation

There was competition, keen competition, but some co-operation did occur. In the autumn of 1929 two of the giants, Orange Luxury and Timpsons, were running their coastal services as a joint operation

An AEC Reliance in the maroon/cream colours of the Royal Arsenal Co-operative Society (RACS), which ran a number of coastal services with picking-up points across South London.

A Leyland Tiger in the small Golden West fleet. The company came under RACS control in the 1930s.

(according to the 'Roadway' timetable), but this only seems to have lasted for one season or at most two. The former company also for a time – this was advertised in 1931 – operated its Great Yarmouth service in conjunction with Norfolk Motor Services, and later withdrew its Southend service, partially at least, when the Carrimore service, (later 'New Karrymore') was diverted to start from the Orange covered station in Brixton.

Following the passage of the 1930 Road Traffic Act, co-operation of a different sort was possible, although the iron hand of the Metropolitan Traffic Commissioner tended to mean that any change had to result in a reduction, if not of facilities, certainly in the number of coaches 'cluttering' the streets. Now, subject to his approval, if an operator wished to withdraw, instead of a mad scramble to pick up his (or her?) custom, there could be an agreed division of the spoils.

When R Neal (Eclipse) withdrew his Ealing-Great

Yarmouth service, the beneficiaries were Grey-Green, United Service Transport and Valliant of Ealing, while when in 1935 Birch Brothers gave up its coastal services from London, established in 1927, it was reported that as many as six other operators gained vehicle allowances and/or picking up points as a result. Principal successors naturally were Grey-Green, Orange Luxury and United Service Transport, but Cronshaws, Venture and Valliant were also involved. Other changes followed a similar pattern.

Not all destinations were served from all scheduled picking-up points, while periods of operation both of basic services and semi-independently of picking up, varied. Some facilities were maintained from Easter to the end of September, some in July and August only. Southend was largely served by day excursions, some even running on Mondays to Fridays only.

While in aggregate the many services ringed Central London, with quite a few penetrating its heart, at least

A Gilford 1680T in the dark red livery of Valliant Coaches (G R and W D Valli). Valliant was the largest coach operator in West London, with a fleet of some 40 coaches in the late 1930s.

A massive-looking Dennis Arrow of Bourne & Balmer (Croydon). A similar coach is seen behind in this garage view.

prior to 1931, overall there was almost incredible variety. Some operators picked up only on line of route with transfers if necessary for different destinations at the final shared point. Alternatively, points might be served in opposite directions for the east and south coasts. Most companies endeavoured to provide through coaches wherever possible, 'Direct daily service: No change of coach' being a powerful selling line, but some perforce ran feeder services, up to as many as seven or eight, converging on a principal interchange, usually the operator's own coach station, which could have toilet and refreshment facilities. Two of them, Blue Belle and United Service Transport, after shedding their higher-frequency services, relied almost exclusively on this arrangement.

One service of Orange Luxury was very different.

This ran every afternoon from Clapham, Victoria, Wood Green etc, to Whipsnade Zoo.

Agents

Another powerful selling point which set the best of the seasonal operators apart from – and above? – the London Coastal group and others, was: 'All seats numbered and reserved'. As their business grew, adding picking-up points and destinations, well-run charting and keen reliable agents were needed. Newsagents/tobacconists, used to high flows of short duration customers, were an obvious choice. Alert agents, while they might also book for competing services of the regional companies (through London Coastal), could have their hidden preferences. Good services produced good commission (agents received

Although not known as a regular picking-up point on the all-year round Empire's Best service from South London via Epping to Colchester and Clacton, this Leyland Tiger was photographed at Eccleston Bridge. Note the most unusual semi-detached drivers cab, a body style made popular by the Arlington Motor Co.

A Maudslay of Eclipse Coaches (R Neal of Acton), also at Eccleston Bridge, a regular picking-up point on this operator's West London-Great Yarmouth service. The passengers do not look at all like bucket-and-spade types!

10-15%) and good agents filled seats. Some did so well that they became almost fully involved with this activity; in many drab outer London streets their shops, windows partly obscured and surrounded by posters, with below a row of brightly coloured billboards, showed up prominently.

In the mid 1930s Timpsons, remaining independent of PSV Operators Ltd (who acted as intermediaries for most operators outside the London Coastal organisation and standardised commission rates) had around 900 agents. All depended on telephone contact with the central chartroom and the regular staff there claimed to know not only all their voices – time was too precious to be wasted on introductions – but also those of their wives and families if they took over fairly often. Booking agents had perforce to keep late hours. Peak demand, as people decided next day's weather would be right for Brighton or perhaps Clacton, was

around 9 to 9.30pm, not long before the second shift in the chartroom, with everything confirmed and documented for drivers on the morning departures, left for home exhausted.

Still on charting, an interesting but unpublicised practice at Rushey Green, the Timpson HQ, was that on morning coastal departures from there the front two nearside seats on each service remained unsold until the very last minute in case any members of the Timpson family wanted a day out!

As indicated earlier, it all began with days out from London, but the smart brightly-coloured coaches dotted around the seaside towns for some hours yielded excellent publicity, and demands arose for journeys originating from the coast, adding to single outward trips. Some of the stronger companies opened booking offices on the coast, with garages and even small coach stations too in the major towns such as

Brighton. Orange Luxury was established in Bournemouth, Brighton, Dover, Eastbourne, Folkestone and Ramsgate, with 'inland' offices at Canterbury and Southampton.

Extra business from the coast was very welcome, filling seats otherwise empty all the way home, but was unpopular with the regional companies running throughout the day with lower average loadings. In the early days of the 1930 Road Traffic Act applications for such extra facilities were bitterly opposed by these companies, led by Southdown Motor Services, and the railways, with the London seasonal operators generally being the losers, despite evidence of past usage. One feature of the existing fare structure which survived was that except in extreme cases, where there might be a difference of 6d, fares were standard from anywhere in London, making South Coast journeys from North London a bargain, with similar benefits for South Londoners going to Clacton etc.

The seasonal operators also lost out in another direction. The Metropolitan Police had long viewed their activities with disfavour, particularly their fondness, born of necessity, for kerbside loading and unloading. As elsewhere a decade or so earlier, regular appearances by large distinctively-coloured vehicles made them an obvious target for complaint, unlike drab delivery vehicles with more flexible schedules. In London however, the cry of excessive road damage could hardly be raised; here the alternative bogey was congestion.

At some points of course congestion was a real problem, for drivers of coaches as well as other road users, and passengers too. The London Coastal terminal was moved from Lower Belgrave Street to a vacant site in Lupus Street, forerunner of Victoria Coach Station, and quite a number of the seasonal operators opened their own off-street stations on the periphery of the central area, but this did not satisfy the authorities. Several of them, including Grey-Green, Orange Luxury and Timpsons, had established picking-up points on the Embankment, but their occasional appearances there were claimed to cause congestion – tell that to King's Ferry and other visitors of recent years – so they were squeezed out. Grey-Green was able to remain with its Felixstowe service until 1933 (Sundays only and late evenings later), and Timpsons hung on until 1939 on Sundays and bank holidays, but many central loading points such as Aldwych, Regent Street and Trafalgar Square were lost, along with many others further from the centre. To be realistic though, some of these had been hurriedly instituted in 1931, presumably in an attempt to beat the deadline, and others were just abandoned.

This points to another problem which must have affected the seasonal services more than those originating in central London. Crude population statistics for inner London boroughs do not reveal much of a shift, but in the 1930s the London County Council made tremendous strides in improving housing for its people by replacing run down property with vast new estates, some of them quite a distance away; the quantitative effects of this on passenger demand are not known.

But despite setbacks, keen competition resulting in well-entrenched low fares and limited use of vehicles, this complex network survived and in the middle to late 1930s it looked healthy. It was however an obvious and immediate wartime casualty – nothing 'essential' about its continued existence – with vehicles then diverted to other and more practical uses. In the summer of 1946 activity was quickly resumed, and by the following year things were in full swing again. This was a time when car ownership was still at a very low level and petrol severely rationed, but when after years

Another sunny day in London. For many years, when custom-built bodywork was common, Orange Luxury favoured sunshine roofs. Clearly this was a day for full opening. The chassis was an AEC Reliance.

A very handsome coach – a Harrington-bodied AEC Regal in the fleet of United Service Transport. The fleetnumber, 614, had real meaning; the combined fleet of coaches, vans and lorries in the late 1930s was in the region of 600.

of austerity the urge to travel was intense. Who though, if given the choice of something better and cheaper, wanted to stand all the way to the seaside on a packed train?

Every coach which ran could be filled, and the future looked bright. I recall an enjoyable outing that summer with a companion, a Scot who marvelled at it all, by Timpsons (the company was by now a BET/Tilling subsidiary), from Blackheath. Our tickets said 'Ramsgate', but we were allowed quite unofficially to disembark at Canterbury, then making our way forward by service bus via Sandwich before rejoining our coach for the return trip. This I am fairly sure was not one of the prewar Harrington dorsal fin bodied AECs, but an equally handsome new Windover-bodied version.

The boom continued, and despite some shrinkage and losses of identity, in c1959 T F McLachlan could still list no fewer than 53 of the survivors providing regular service facilities from the Metropolitan Police District to enable thousands, nay tens or even hundreds of thousands on the busiest day of the year

(the same author gives a figure of 14,000 for Margate alone) to escape the dust and clamour of London for a day at the seaside.

It is not my intention to chart the later and declining fortunes of the London seasonal operators, but I feel that their contribution to London life over half a century and more should not be entirely forgotten.

The hardware

To go into detail about the many vehicles employed at times by the London seasonal operators, or even to provide an adequate summary, is likewise beyond the scope of this article. Divergences of opinions and policies, adding to varying capacity requirements, make generalisations difficult.

The earliest ones were of course charabancs or even platform lorries with minimal modifications, solid tyred. Pneumatics followed, leaving London's buses behind, and 'all-weather' coaches, before hard tops took over. Full-sized coaches (32 seaters or larger) were preferred, although some concerns, eg Julius and Lockwood and one of the largest, Orange Luxury,

Vehicles like this caused quite a stir at the time of their first appearance. A London Lorries-bodied AEC Regal observation coach of Blue Belle.

relied to a large extent on all-weather Bedfords once this make became available.

I began by stressing how clean and well-kept were the coaches I saw in the middle to late 1930s; this does not mean they were all the latest models, Blue Belle and Timpsons perhaps excepted. Regional bus companies could do better, by downgrading their express coaches fairly quickly to less-demanding duties and replacing by new, but this option was not available in the London seasonal fleets. Annual mileages too tended to be lower, giving longer trouble-free life. However, following behind the extended tour operators, their vehicles did tend to appear for sale earlier than many.

Combining lightness and speed, Gilfords were a popular choice in the heyday of that make, Maudslays and a few Tilling Stevens too, with a fair sprinkling before and after of many other well-known makes. The Leyland name was well represented, but in the part of London I was most familiar with, AECs predominated. The Grey-Green fleet was mixed, as were those of Orange Luxury and United Service Transport, but in the mid-1930s that of Blue Belle was 100% AEC, with Timpsons almost the same. The former had some very handsome London Lorries-bodied observation coaches, a rarity these, while in the latter's fleet Harrington bodies, including the famous dorsal fin types, seemed to be in the majority. A few years earlier the Blue Belle fleet was stated to comprise 40 Regals and 10 Commer Invaders, whereas that of Timpsons, while 70% of AEC manufacture, had representatives of eight other makes in the total of 174. This last figure, it should be added, must have included vehicles based outside London, at Hastings, Ramsgate and Torquay.

When needed fleet replacement started after the War Bedfords were one of the most readily available makes, their producer having gained from continuing wartime production of the OWB, but many London buyers returned to heavier chassis as soon as they could. The Timpson company, in line with its new-found associates, continued this policy, but as larger-capacity Bedfords were built they began to appear in London in appreciable numbers: this may have indicated a lingering bias in favour of petrol engines. The Orange Luxury fleet, it is understood, when acquired by Ewers, comprised some 50 Bedfords, mostly OBs; the 30-strong fleet of Fallowfield & Britten, taken over by Ewers in the previous year (1952), was also predominantly of Bedford manufacture.

But in customer terms, most important whatever enthusiasts may think, careful study of fleet lists cannot present a true picture. Vehicles actually in use at busy summer weekends far outnumbered the total owned by the licensed operators. To meet demand substantial hiring was imperative; the Home Counties were scoured for coaches, with drivers of course, and top quality was sometimes difficult to achieve. Passengers expecting a Timpson coach to appear could be critical when faced with an unfamiliar livery, not always perhaps without justification. This was a problem few operators, in London or elsewhere, did not have to face at some time or another. ∎

Acknowledgments

I am indebted to Mr T F McLachlan FCIT, who read through my original draft, providing a number of helpful comments and corrections, and to Mr R G Westgate, who gave me several items of valuable information about London coaching matters. Further and more detailed accounts of some aspects of the subject may be found in the following: Independent Express Services from London to the Coast (T F McLachlan, published by The Omnibus Society c1959). This publication includes a more authoritative summary of the types of vehicle in use at this time and a little earlier. The Grey-Green Story (T F McLachlan, published by The Omnibus Society c1963). By the same author, this is a detailed history to that date of the company which led the London coach field for many years. Francis Flin and MT(Motor Coaches) Ltd (Frank Woodworth MCIT, The Omnibus Magazine No 384, June/July 1992).

WARTIME IN WEST CUMBERLAND

Schoolboy memories of unfrozen, secondhand, utility and rebodied buses by HARRY POSTLETHWAITE

A postwar photo with a wartime flavour showing the 'temporary' building which replaced the Grand Hotel. Also shown is Bedford OWB No 23, Leyland TD2 No 156 with Northern Coachbuilders body, and Billy Sim's Bedford OB, with which he operated a market day service from Eskdale to Whitehaven. Visible behind is the roof of the former carriage sheds at Whitehaven's Bransty station and behind that the Quaker Oats building.

Cumberland Motor Services

I WAS BORN in Whitehaven in 1934 and from the earliest age which I can remember took a great interest in the activities of the local bus company, Cumberland Motor Services Ltd (CMS). Whitehaven was a 'bus town' with a substantial covered bus station, head office of CMS, a three-storey engineering building and a depot/workshop building all situated together at the northern approach to the town centre.

The fleet at the outbreak of World War 2 was a conservative one where double-deckers, all of lowbridge pattern, predominated. There were two Massey-bodied AEC Regents but the remainder were all Leylands of TD1, TD3, TD4 or TD5 types. Apart from two TD5s in the 1939 delivery with East Lancashire Coachbuilders bodies, the remainder were bodied by either Leyland or Massey. Heavyweight single-deckers were Leyland or AEC with bodies by Leyland, Massey or Burlingham plus a Duple-bodied AEC Regal taken over with the business of a local operator in Carlisle. In addition there were a number of lightweight single-deckers including a number of Commers supplied by Myers & Bowman Ltd of Distington who were Commer main agents.

The service pattern comprised trunk routes from

Whitehaven to Carlisle, Whitehaven to Keswick, and from Whitehaven to Millom, plus an extensive network of services concentrated in West Cumberland. This was the scene in 1939.

The war was to have no obvious effect on the delivery of new vehicles for the first two years, but the effect on services was almost immediate as restrictions on the supply of fuel brought about reductions in services. The twice-yearly timetable booklets were replaced by two folded sheets, one covering the 'Northern Section' (services north of Whitehaven) and the other covering the 'Southern Section' (services south of Whitehaven). These were priced at one penny each and the first was effective from 7 October 1939. Some services were withdrawn and Sunday operation became very restricted. Table 1 gives details of the services included in the timetables dated 21 December 1939. These timetables were revised as and when fuel supplies worsened or eased.

West Cumberland was regarded as a 'safe area' during the war with very limited effects from bombing and as a result of this evacuees from many parts of the country were brought into the area. The industrial base of the area expanded with the establishment of Royal Ordnance factories at Drigg and Sellafield, the High Duty Alloys Ltd factory at Distington and an armaments depot at Broughton Moor. Further afield but still within the company operating area, there were RAF stations at Silloth, Orton, Kirkbride and Haverigg and a RNAS station at Anthorn. All these combined to place additional demands on Cumberland Motor Services Ltd.

Acquired vehicles

In early 1940 six Leyland TD1s, with standard Leyland lowbridge bodies, arrived having previously served with Wilts & Dorset Motor Services Ltd. All had commenced life with other operators and details are given on page 124. Whilst I have no recollection of the arrival of these vehicles, I do remember them well. Three of them, Nos 148-50 had Gardner 5LW engines fitted and had their bodies reconditioned by East Lancs before entering service. These together with No 151, which was purchased later in the year from Yorkshire Traction Co. Ltd, spent almost their entire time with CMS on the Workington town service to Harrington and the local service from Workington to Seaton. The thing which distinguished them from other TD1s was that they had the large-type destination aperture, as introduced in the mid-1930s, rather than the single-line type fitted to the other TD1s. The other three vehicles of this batch received new bodies as detailed later.

I do have a vague recollection of being taken into town one Saturday and seeing some strange vehicles operating on Whitehaven town services. They were numbered 152-8 and I was to learn later that they had come from London Transport and were Leyland TD2 models, one being bodied by Birch and the others by Dodson. They had arrived with London Transport from a variety of small operators and as such were non-standard in the fleet. They were completely different to anything in the CMS fleet and being of highbridge pattern, precautions had to be taken to ensure they did not operate on a route where there

Top: **CMS Nos 154/6, ex-London Transport Leyland TD2s with open-staircase bodies stand in the New Road garage, Whitehaven. Alongside is No 86, one of the ex-Southdown TD1s with Short Bros body.**
S L Poole

Above: **Typical of the five ex-London Transport Dodson-bodied TD2s is No 153 standing outside the Whitehaven depot building (often referred to as the '1932 workshops'). Despite showing Hensingham on the destination blind, it was in fact** *en route* **from Hensingham to Bransty. It was policy in those days not to change destination blinds on local journeys.**
S L Poole

Also Bransty bound, in spite of the destination, is No 154 after being rebodied by Northern Coachbuilders.
The location is the same as for No 153, the bus station stop for the Bransty service

S L Poole

One of the Park Royal-bodied Leyland TD7s, No 172, built for Southdown and diverted to Cumberland on completion, seen *en route* from Keswick to Whitehaven.

S L Poole

was a low bridge. A prominent notice was displayed in the driver's cab and on the platform declaring: DOUBLE DECK BUS 14ft 6in HIGH. Not to be operated on Frizington, Cleator-Egremont, Seaton, Harrington-Workington routes. Two of them had open-staircase bodies and these together with other acquired open-staircase buses fascinated the local schoolboys as CMS had disposed of its open-staircase-bodied TD1s in 1936. The fascination was however short-lived as all received new bodies in 1943. The other five received Gardner 5LW engines and spent most of their time on Whitehaven town services where there were no low bridges. Another feature of these vehicles was the 'half-door' fitted to the driver's cab, the upper portion being a fold-up blind which, even when rolled down was anything but draughtproof and did nothing to endear these vehicles to the drivers, particularly in winter.

The next used vehicles were five Leyland TD1 models with lowbridge Leyland or Cowieson bodies from Glasgow Corporation Transport. All had been fitted with Leyland 8.6 litre diesel engines whilst with Glasgow and this made them unique in the CMS fleet as the only vehicles of that vintage to have this engine. The other lasting memory of these vehicles is that they were very dilapidated and all but one (No 62) were rebodied. I suspect that No 62 had its body extensively reconditioned as I recall it being in reasonable condition and having proprietary sliding ventilators in some side windows; there is however nothing in the

records to confirm this. At least some of these operated for a time in the Glasgow livery. Shortly after this, two Leyland TD1s arrived from Preston Corporation, one with standard Leyland lowbridge open-staircase body and the other with a highbridge English Electric body. Both operated in the Preston livery but I have no clear recollection of the latter vehicle and both were rebodied, the former receiving a Gardner 5LW engine at the same time.

I do recall being told that there were some 'green buses' operating in the town and these turned out to be a batch of six Leyland TD1s and three Leyland TD2s with Short Bros. highbridge bodies from Southdown. The TD2s were fitted with Gardner 5LW engines and were set to work on Whitehaven town services alongside the ex-London Transport TD2s. I still remember being impressed by the interiors of these vehicles, standard Southdown seating covered in brown moquette trimmed with brown leather and the superb Southdown livery which remained a favourite with me from that time. These buses arrived in September 1940 and the only other used vehicles to be acquired were three Guy FCX with Short Bros open-top bodies from Morecambe & Heysham Corporation and a number of single-deckers, mainly lightweight, purchased with the businesses of local operators. The three Guy FCX were acquired in 1942 for works transport within the Royal Ordinance Factory at Drigg and were rarely seen elsewhere.

New vehicles

The year 1941 saw the arrival of the first new vehicles for two years and these comprised 15 Leyland TD7 double-deckers. Five had Massey bodies and five had East Lancs bodies all obviously built to the same specification, although I always considered that the Massey bodies were the more stylish of the two. They were the first vehicles in the fleet to have service number indicators and these comprised twin-track blinds at the front alongside the standard large destination/intermediate point display and a similar arrangement at the side alongside a deep single-line blind. On the Massey bodies this side arrangement was above the rearmost window but on the East Lancashire bodies it was above the platform. The interior finish was to the Cumberland standard with brown leather-covered seating in tubular chrome-plated frames, brown leathercloth-covered interior panels and polished wood to the window surrounds and to the upper portion of the lower saloon bulkhead. They had the familiar Clayton Dewandre circular heaters on the lower saloon and upper saloon bulkheads and they were excellent vehicles.

Another four of these TD7s caused me something of a problem for although the chassis were, as far as I could tell, similar to the other ten, the bodies were completely different. There was no visible bodybuilder's nameplate so I was unable to identify the builder and apart from the body shape there were two obvious differences to the others. The destination displays comprised a large aperture at both front and rear with no side display and no provision for service numbers, and the seating was covered in brown moquette trimmed with brown leather. It was this last factor which gave me a clue for I noticed some similarity between this seating and that in the ex-Southdown vehicles. With all the wisdom of a seven-year-old I concluded that they must have been built by the same bodybuilder, Short Brothers of Rochester. It was many years later that I learned that these bodies had been built by Park Royal for Southdown, to its specification, and diverted to Cumberland on completion. At least I derived come satisfaction from the fact that my detective work as a seven-year-old did conclude with some element of truth in that there was after all a link with Southdown. The final vehicle in this batch of 15 arrived late in the year and whilst the body outline was unmistakably Massey, it was devoid of all frills, with square corners to the windows, lack of lining panels and with simplified seating. It was followed in 1942 by another TD7 but this had a body by Northern Counties, a make hitherto unknown to me but at least the builder was identified. It was many years later that I learned that these vehicles were classified as 'unfrozen'. One of the Massey-bodied TD7s, No 162 was unfortunately extensively damaged by fire in 1943 and received a new Northern Coachbuilders body in 1944.

The utilities

At this time we lived in the south side of Whitehaven but the school had been condemned and we were taken by bus to a school in the north side of the town.

An unfrozen Leyland TD7, No 176, photographed when new by the bodybuilder, Massey Bros. Note the lack of white relief to the grey livery, apart from the edges to the mudguard and guardrail.

The school bus did not travel via the town centre but as I had taken a dislike to school dinners I travelled home each lunchtime on the service bus which meant that I passed the bus station twice a day and was able to keep up to date with developments. It was early in 1943 that I noticed two strange double-deckers in the depot. They had austere-looking bodies and unfamiliar radiators, closer examination of which revealed the word 'GUY' at the top. This came as something of a surprise to a nine-year-old who thought that all buses were manufactured by either Leyland or AEC. There had been a Guy double-decker in the fleet, an FCX, but this had been disposed of in 1935 and also two single-deckers which had likewise departed by 1935. The two new Guys were followed by three more all with lowbridge bodies, the maker of which did not appear to be identified. They were very utility, having square-cornered windows without window pans, no lining panels, were devoid of curves and had rather spartan brown leather-covered seating with very low backs. It was some years later that I learned that the bodies were by Brush Coachworks.

There were three other similar-bodied vehicles but they had different radiators, without manufacturer's name but with fluted top. Someone whose father worked for CMS told me they were Daimlers and that they had funny gearboxes with the operating lever mounted on the steering column. CMS attempted to negotiate with Lancaster City Transport for the exchange of these Daimlers in return for two Guys and one Leyland TD7, in the interests of standardisation for both parties, but nothing came of this.

Among these Brush-bodied vehicles another Guy had appeared with a different body but this was identified as built by Northern Counties. The austerity in this case was reduced slightly by the use of window pans with radiused bottom corners. On this and the next two similar bodies the seating was covered in red leather but of rather spartan design which I remember as being distinctly uncomfortable. Another 11 similar-bodied Guys arrived but these had the infamous slatted wooden seats. The final two Guys arrived in 1944 and had Massey bodies with slatted wooden seats but retained the polished timber finish to the upper portion of the lower saloon bulkhead and this went some way towards relieving the utility specification.

The only other new vehicles to be received during wartime were single-deck Bedford OWB type with the standard utility body designed for this vehicle. The first two for Cumberland were built by SMT and arrived in 1943. They were followed in 1944 by another 11 and in

1945 by a further two, all with Duple bodies. I must admit that I never regarded normal-control buses as being 'proper buses' but having said that these lightweights did seem to give reasonable service on a variety of routes, mainly rural.

Whilst the Guys were arriving, Northern Coachbuilders was busy providing new bodies on a variety of reconditioned Leyland TD1 and TD2 chassis. These bodies had their own character and certainly had the most substantial seating, with brown leather covering, of any of the utility double-deckers. This was rather ironic because, being on older chassis, they tended to be used on shorter services. The seating arrangement upstairs was unusual in that there were alternate rows for three and four passengers, the idea being to give the conductor somewhere to stand whilst he was collecting fares and passengers were attempting to alight. The reduction in seating capacity was compensated for by an additional row of seats. The bodybuilder was clearly identified by a transfer on the lower saloon bulkhead and details of the vehicles concerned are given in tables 2 and 5. The only single-deckers to receive new bodies were four Leyland TS1s which received the standard wartime body produced by H V Burlingham Ltd.

No 217 was one of the Massey-bodied Guy Arab IIs, and is shown at Flatt Walks, Whitehaven, outside the old hospital. The body had been rebuilt with rubber-mounted windows without detracting from the familiar Massey wartime body outline. It was unique among rebuilt CMS wartime Guys in not being provided with service number blinds.

A B Cross

Something borrowed

The interest of this young enthusiast and others like him, was further advanced with the arrival of numerous vehicles on hire. These included London Transport ST types complete with anti-shatter material on the windows and a Leyland TD1 from Manchester Corporation Transport which I can still picture travelling down High Road, Kells, and carrying the number 215. There were green AEC Regents from Morecambe & Heysham Corporation Transport, maroon Leylands from Bolton Corporation Transport and dark red Leylands from East Kent. All added to the variety and interest of the transport scene in West Cumberland at that time.

All vehicles eventually received the wartime livery of grey with limited white relief, normally two bands in the case of double-deckers, and with a CMS monogram in place of the CUMBERLAND fleetname.

The allocation of vehicles to services was consistent, with the TD7s working the longer distances particularly Whitehaven- Carlisle and Keswick, supplemented as necessary by the Brush-bodied Guy Arab Is and sometimes by TD5s. The Northern Counties-bodied Guy Arab IIs together with the TD4s and TD5s worked the intermediate-length services such as Whitehaven – Thornhill, Frizington; Maryport – Cockermouth, and Workington – Cockermouth. Whitehaven town services were worked by the ex-London Transport and Southdown TD2s supplemented by rebodied Gardner-engined TD1s and TD2s. In Workington, where there were low bridges on the services to Harrington and Seaton, the local services were operated by Gardner-engined acquired TD1s supplemented by two of the original CMS TD1s, Nos.105/7 which had received Gardner engines and new Northern Coachbuilders bodies. Petrol-engined vehicles were normally restricted to works and other occasional services.

The fleet had grown considerably during wartime and this would have created an accommodation problem at Whitehaven had it not been for a rather unfortunate incident. The Grand Hotel, which was situated adjacent to the bus station, was destroyed by fire on 21 January 1940 and the site was purchased by CMS. A 'temporary' building was erected, which incidentally lasted until 1991, and was used together with the surrounding area for the parking of buses.

That other infamous relic of wartime days, the producer gas trailer, appeared on the scene, a total of 21 being obtained. There are no details of the vehicles to which they were fitted but they did not prove to be satisfactory on Whitehaven's hills and were generally used in the Workington and Maryport areas.

This was the scene in wartime West Cumberland. In many ways they were dark days. No road lighting, masked headlights and masked interior lighting to vehicles, restrictions on many things but nevertheless very interesting days for a young bus enthusiast when one had to glean information from whatever source one could, usually school friends whose father worked for the CMS, for there was no *Buses Illustrated* in those days.

Northern Counties-bodied Guy Arab II No 213 stands alongside the Maryport depot building in the postwar years, after rebuilding with single-line destination indicator and service number blinds.

Cumberland Motor Services

They were difficult days in other respects too. An ageing fleet was deteriorating, both mechanically and bodily. It was a common sight to see the mobile battery pack being wheeled out of the depot to a bus which would not start and by the end of the war body deterioration was evident on many buses, particularly those which had not been rebodied or received major rebuilding. The ex-London Transport and Southdown vehicles suffered noticeably in this respect. Although the war finished in 1945 it was early 1947 before the first signs of major fleet renewal appeared, but that is another interesting story. ■

The author acknowledges the value of the PSV Circle Fleet History for Cumberland Motor Services in providing detailed information on the vehicles. Photographs by S L Poole and that from the A B Cross collection are reproduced by kind permission of Mr A B Cross. Thanks are also expressed to the Friends of Whitehaven Museum for permission to use its photograph and to Cumberland Motor Services for the use of photographs from its collection. The help of Mr Brian Pritchard in checking the text and providing helpful comment is gratefully acknowledged.

VEHICLES ACQUIRED IN WARTIME FROM OTHER OPERATORS

Leyland TD1: Wilts & Dorset TM 3736, VW 8823, RU 9494, CK 4208, CM 8726/9. Yorkshire Traction HE 4976. Glasgow Corporation GE 2403/99, 7200/4/5. Preston Corporation CK 4172/4602. Southdown UF 8373-6/81/3.

Leyland TD2: London Transport GW 550, GY 2042, HV 2822, EV 5860/6510/8335, GW 1285. Southdown UF 8844/5/8.

Guy FCX: Morecambe & Heysham TD 2718/9,7135.

VEHICLES ON LOAN DURING WARTIME

Bolton Corporation: WH 5504 (Leyland TD3c), WH 6863 (Leyland TD4c), WH 9218/9/22 (Leyland TD5c).

East Kent JG 1622-4 (Leyland TD1).

London Transport GF 404/7247, GH 556/8071, GK 3008 (AEC Regent).

Manchester Corporation VR 6004 (Leyland TD1).

Morecambe & Heysham TF 7468-70, TJ 2490/1 (AEC Regent).

NEW VEHICLES PURCHASED IN WARTIME

Bedford OWB/Duple FAO 282/3, 505-10, 686-90.

Bedford OWB/SMT ERM 680/1.

Daimler CWG5/Brush ERM 677-9.

Guy Arab I/Brush ERM 672-6.

Guy Arab II/Northern Counties ERM 910-4, FAO 51-8.

Guy Arab II/Massey FAO 59/60.

Leyland TD7/Massey EAO 699-703, ERM 127.

Leyland TD7/East Lancs EAO 704-8.

Leyland TD7/Park Royal EAO 724-7.

Leyland TD7/Northern Counties ERM 128.

CUMBERLAND MOTOR SERVICES
Bus routes 21 December 1939

Southern Section

Whitehaven-Egremont-Seascale-Millom (daily)

Whitehaven-Cleator Moor-Frizington-Lamplugh (daily)

Whitehaven-Cleator Moor-Cleator-Egremont (Mon-Sat)

Whitehaven-Cleator Moor-Rowrah-Cockermouth (Mon/Sat)

Whitehaven-Cleator Moor-Ennerdale-Cockermouth (Mon/Thu)

Whitehaven-Cleator Moor-Ennerdale Bridge (Sat)

Whitehaven-St Bees (Mon-Sat)

Whitehaven-Moor Row (Mon-Sat)

Whitehaven-Moresby Parks-Pica (Mon-Sat)

Whitehaven-Kells (town service) (Mon-Sat)

Whitehaven-Woodhouse (town service) (Mon-Sat)

Bransty-Whitehaven-Hensingham Square (town service) Mon-Sat)

Millom-The Green (Sun/Mon/Thu/Sat)

Northern Section

Whitehaven-Workington-Aspatria-Wigton-Carlisle (daily)

Whitehaven-Workington-Silloth-Wigton-Carlisle (daily)

Whitehaven-Lowca-Workington (daily)

Whitehaven-Workington-Cockermouth-Keswick (daily)

Carlisle-Wigton-Keswick (not Thu)

Carlisle-Wigton-Cockermouth (Mon-Sat)

Workington-Clifton (Mon-Sat)

Workington-Seaton (Mon-Sat)

Workington-Harrington (town service) (daily)

Workington-Little Broughton (Sat)

Workington-Dean (Sat)

Maryport-Dearham-Cockermouth (Mon-Sat)

Maryport-Allonby-Wigton (Tue)

Cockermouth-Aspatria (Mon/Sat)

Cockermouth-Little Broughton (Mon/Sat)

Cockermouth-Blindcrake (Mon)

Cockermouth-Loweswater (schooldays)

Cockermouth-Buttermere (Mon)

Aspatria-Bothel-Wigton (schooldays)

Uldale-Wigton (Tue)

Wigton-Aikton-Oulton-Carlisle (Mon/Tue.Sat)

Wigton-Langrigg-Westnewton (Tue)

Wigton-Mealgate-Aspatria (Mon-Sat)

CLASSIC BUS ALPHABET

S IS FOR STOP, the word printed in large enough white capitals to be able to be read by conductors and drivers changing the route numbers of buses with multi-track blinds. We can only surmise that there were some unfortunate mishaps in the early days of these blinds, and crews turned the handles with such unrestrained vigour that the number scrolls were wrenched off their spindles. Whatever the reason, 'STOP' was printed to about half the depth of the numbers and appeared at the beginning and end of the scroll to warn crews to stop turning. No problem in that, but instead of being a discreet instruction just for the uniformed employee clinging perilously to the bonnet of their bus, too often it was displayed to the world as part of the route number. So displays like this Western SMT 'STOP 36' could be accompanied by a '3 STOP 6', '36 STOP' and other more confusing permutations like 'X3 STOP – EXPRESS' or 'STOP STOP STOP – LIMITED STOP'. Progress, internally operated blinds and electronic destination displays have put a stop to 'STOP'.

T IS FOR TIGER. Tiger Coaches, that is. This Tiger Coaches didn't actually run any coaches. It was in the 1950s and 1960s the last resting place of many of Glasgow Corporation's withdrawn buses. Glasgow's buses were worked hard and few were fit for further service by the time they were withdrawn.

Instead they made one final journey to the great bus garage in the sky – and Tiger Coaches was one of the routes which they took. Based in Salsburgh, midway between Glasgow and Edinburgh, the company scrapped prewar and postwar buses from Glasgow – and from elsewhere too, usually in Scotland, but occasionally from south of the border.

The Tiger name was also used for a single-deck chassis by a well-known manufacturer, but that's another tale.

U IS FOR UNDERFLOOR, where postwar single-deck manufacturers decided to bung the engine, out of the way. Leyland and AEC were in the race to build the first underfloor-engined buses after the war, but were probably so busy watching each other suspiciously that they never thought to keep an eye on Sentinel, which romped home with an underfloor-engined bus in 1948, in an integral structure by Beadle. Sentinel indeed had only just discovered internal combustion, and had been slinging steam engines under the floor of lorries for some time; perhaps it never occurred to it to turn the cylinders the right way up when it started building diesels. BMMO also built early underfloor-engined buses, and built the first successful underfloor-engined double-deckers, though AEC had built one, the Regent IV, with less success in the 1950s. While in single-deckers there was a capacity benefit, there was little benefit in double-deckers, given how high the floorline had to be. Some would say underfloor-engined designs spelt the end of the classic bus.

V IS FOR VIKING. Albion's last-ditch attempt to build a bus chassis to keep the Scottish Bus Group happy. Launched with a front engine in 1963, the Viking resurfaced two years later with its Leyland 400 engine mounted at the rear. SBG, which didn't go a bundle on rear-engined single-deckers, preferring the trusty underfloor-engined Leopard, bought the Viking in respectable numbers as a lightweight replacement for the last of its halfcabs. Not the most sophisticated of buses, the Viking gave good service to SBG companies and to the many overseas buyers. Leyland used Glasgow-based Albion to produce chassis to meet SBG's vehicle requirements, which tended to be, er, different to those of other operators. Hence the Nimbus, Aberdonian, Lowlander and Viking, but the Viking was to be the last.

W IS FOR WIGHT (ISLE OF). As a nation of islanders, we love even smaller islands and south of a line from the Midlands to the Wash, the Isle of Wight acts as a magnet in the same way as others are drawn to the Isle of Man or some of the Scottish islands. While those northerly islands' bus interest was in their independence, the Isle of Wight had its own Tilling/National Bus Company fleet in Southern Vectis. This added to the 'England in miniature' appeal of the island, as its picture postcard villages and narrow lanes were served by a self-contained, almost toytown fleet of big company buses – K-types, Lodekkas, MWs, even VRs and REs, all painted immaculately and working at their hardest on routes for happy holidaymakers. Reputedly, Southern Vectis earned its profits in the summer and used them to keep its all-year-round routes going in the winter. And we can well believe there was more than the occasional visiting enthusiast who imagined himself in the seemingly idyllic role of general manager of

A Bedford/Duple coach and a Southern Vectis Bristol/ECW Lodekka feature on this Wight (Isle of) postcard.

Southern Vectis, able to put his feet up while the buses ran like clockwork and the profits piled up predictably. No doubt the real general managers dreamed of a similarly idyllic existence when they wrestled with their daily grind, but the enthusiast's happy misconception was (and still is) part of the island's magic.

X IS A DIFFICULT LETTER. Xanadu & District Motor Services? Sounds unlikely. Xavier, the well-known Spanish coach operator? Pushing it a bit . . . XTC, the 1980s pop group? Well, just about. Add a few numbers to it – say 209. No, not 209, try 684. (This doesn't work with all pop group names, incidentally. The Dave Clark Five 684 is, we suspect, devoid of meaning.) But add 684 to XTC and what do you get? Firstly, a sneaky way out of the letter X conundrum. And secondly, hey presto!: XTC 684, a famous bus.

It was, of course, the second of Leyland's two Low-loader prototypes, the precursor to the Atlantean. It had a halfcab Metro-Cammell body and an open rear platform, an unlikely layout for a model which was about to revolutionise urban transport in Britain. The engine was mounted in the rear offside corner. XTC 684 was used as a demonstrator, then ran for a period with Lowland Motorways in Glasgow before ending up being saved for preservation.

An Albion *Viking* VK43L with Alexander *Y-type* bodywork.

Y IS FOR Y-TYPE. Alexander (says one of the few writers of this alphabet who's never been in public relations for a coach builder) has a funny approach to bus design. Sometimes it comes up with a design which is a real classic. Sometimes it comes up with a design which – er – isn't. When you see some of the bodies in the latter category, you wonder how on earth it ever managed to produce one of the best-looking and most versatile single-deckers of the 1960s, a design it carried on for over 20 years. The Y-type still didn't look out of place at the end of its run, when it was replaced by a garden shed called the P-type.

As a mark of its versatility, the Y-type began life in 1961 as a futuristic multi-door urban bus for Edinburgh, yet within a few years was being used on front-line coach work from that fair city to London. It established Alexander outside Scotland, becoming a sort of honorary BET-type with a wide range of operators, and even going to some English municipalities, such as Bury on AEC Reliances and Lincoln on Bristol REs, and independents such as Premier Travel (AEC Reliances again). All sorts of chassis carried Y-types, including Britain's first Volvo, Leylands, AECs, Albions, Bristols, Bedfords, Fords, Seddons – and even a Volvo B57 and a Dennis Lancet.

Z IS FOR, ER, DUAL PURPOSE. Scottish Motor Traction, SMT, used simple letter codes for its fleet. So B was AEC (illogical, I know, but A had already been used for Albion and was later used for Bristol), H was Leyland (don't ask), and so on. For a while double-deckers were given similar codes (E was Guy, J was Leyland) but then somebody reckoned that a double-deck AEC should be BB, a double-deck Bristol AA – you get the drift – so that depot controllers and inspectors could easily distinguish single-deckers and double-deckers and allocate them accordingly. Then somebody realised that single-deck AECs – Bs – could be buses, coaches or toilet-fitted coaches. So buses continued as Bs, toilet-fitted coaches became XBs, touring coaches became YBs and dual-purpose vehicles became ZBs. On reflection it might have been easier simply to run off a few more fleetlists for the controllers, but for a while Eastern Scottish buses carried fleetnumbers that took up a substantial part of the front panels. Oh yes – there was a suffix to distinguish the depot allocation. It had its equivalent of A for Bristol and B for AEC: Dalkeith was G and Galashiels D. (See also under N.)